# VIOLENCE IN FACTUAL TELEVISION

## Annual Review 1993

*Edited by*

Andrea Millwood Hargrave

*BROADCASTING STANDARDS COUNCIL*
*PUBLIC OPINION AND BROADCASTING STANDARDS – 4*

John Libbey

JL

LONDON · PARIS · ROME

British Library Cataloguing in Publication Data

Violence and Factual Television. –
   Public Opinion & Broadcasting Standards
   (ISSN 0960-3999; Vol. 4)

   I. Hargrave, Andrea Millwood   II. Series
   384.54

ISSN:  0960-3999
ISBN: 0 86196 441 1

Published by

**John Libbey & Company Ltd,** 13 Smiths Yard, Summerley Street,
London SW18 4HR, England
**Telephone: 081-947 2777 – Fax: 081-947 2664**
**John Libbey Eurotext Ltd,** 6 rue Blanche, 92120 Montrouge, France
**John Libbey - C.I.C. s.r.l.,** via Lazzaro Spallanzani 11, 00161 Rome, Italy

Printed in Great Britain by Whitstable Litho Ltd, Whitstable, Kent, UK

# VIOLENCE IN FACTUAL TELEVISION

*BROADCASTING STANDARDS COUNCIL*

5-8 The Sanctuary
London SW1P 3JS

Tel: 071-233 0544
Fax: 071-233 0397

# Contents

# Foreword

This is the fourth in the series of Annual Reviews conducted by the Broadcasting Standards Council since its creation in 1988. Each Review deals with a different aspect of the principal concerns in the Council's remit: violence, sexual conduct, and matters of taste and decency. The first, published in 1990, reported on *Violence in Television Fiction*, describing responses among the audience to the different kinds of violence displayed in programmes and developing the concept of 'Deep Play' and 'Shallow Play' to measure the relative depth of the audience's involvement.

The choice as the subject for 1993 of Violence in Factual Television has a particular topicality. First, because of the existence throughout the world of conflicts, often small-scale, but no less bloody for that and each one of them capable of being brought almost instantly into the home by faster and faster means of news delivery. Secondly, because of the sharp rise during the year of anxieties, in Britain as elsewhere in the world, about the effects on the audience of their exposure to violence on the screen.

The Council, in addition to commissioning MORI Ltd. to conduct quantitative research for the Review, welcomed the opportunity to enrich the debate by commissioning research of a rather different kind from the Institute of Communications Studies at the University of Leeds. This enabled a number of ordinary viewers, by acting as their own editors, to give a series of fresh perspectives on the attitudes of the audience normally watching passively at home. Their responses to this opportunity provide interesting questions for those who have to deal with the same problems professionally day by day. The Council would like to express its appreciation for the willingness of the BBC, ITN and Sky News to make material available for this research. Without it, nothing so comprehensive could have been attempted.

Finally, as the Council did in association with its earlier surveys on Bad Language and Sex & Sexuality, it asked a group of contributors, most of them professionally involved in the broadcasting of factual programmes, to express their own opinions on the issues covered by the 1993 survey.

This is the first Annual Review to be published since I became Chairman of the Council and I welcome the opportunity of renewing the Council's strong commitment to the importance of its research activities as the foundation for its other work. I hope that *Violence in Factual Television* will stimulate the discussion, both beyond the broadcasting industry and within it, of matters of considerable importance to society now and for the future.

Lady Howe
*Chairman*
*Broadcasting Standards Council*

# Introduction

Innovative, sound and independent research has been a cornerstone of the work of the Broadcasting Standards Council. Not only is the commissioning of it a key element of the remit, but it provides essential support to the Council's function as a body which considers complaints about broadcasting from the audience. The research itself is strengthened and amplified by evidence collected through consultations and meetings held with members of this audience.

As noted in the Foreword, the Council and other bodies have conducted research into the depiction of violence in fictional television. There has been very little published of comparative depth which considers factual programmes. This is, of course, an important area of the Council's remit. It becomes of increasing importance with the rise in reconstruction programmes and those that use the fly-on-the-wall style of filming. There are also now channels offering 24 hour news, collected quickly and with the pressure to transmit equally quickly.

The Annual Review was constructed therefore, to attempt to answer the following questions: Do people distinguish between fiction and factual programmes? Is there a blurring at the edges – 'faction programming' – with the increased use of reconstructions forming the central content of programmes in their own right and, for example, in documentaries? Previous research has shown the importance of the relationship between programme genre and context – is this relationship deemed important in factual programming? How does this relationship affect attitudes to actual content? What is the effect of respondents' own experiences of violence and how do their concerns about violence in society impact on their attitudes to violent images in factual television? (Research conducted by the Council in 1990 had shown that nearly a third of respondents thought that British society was 'extremely' or 'very' violent. Only 11 per cent said that it was 'not very violent'.)

The 1993 survey tested in detail people's attitudes to violent material in each of news, reconstruction programmes and documentaries. The first stage used the traditional qualitative technique of group discussions among people recruited on the basis of similar demographic or other characteristics. But it also included a pioneering technique developed by the Institute of Communications Studies at the University of Leeds which asked these respondents to consider the way in which they might edit the material they were shown. This technique allowed the respondent to separate different elements in the television reports such as picture, voice-over, dialogue, sequencing of events and allowed the researchers to analyse in detail the attitudes and considerations that drove these decisions. Respondents were given access both to transmitted and untransmitted material. A similar technique had been used in the Council's consideration of violence in television fiction (1990); and had proved the importance of context to the respondent, as well as the need for purpose or relevance when violent images were shown.

These findings were very much amplified by the editing groups (reported on in full in Section 2) in this Annual Review. From the analysis of the results, a series of hypotheses was created to provide a framework of 'acceptability' for viewing factual material. In brief, these hypotheses stated (i) that the viewer required 'certainty' about the outcome of an event; (ii) that the 'closeness' of the event to the viewer's own world and experience enhanced the disturbance caused to the viewer; (iii) that the 'status' of the victim in the viewer's mind was central to the viewer's reaction to the event – the greater the sympathy the viewer had with the victim or victims, the more upset the viewer would be ; and finally (iv) the event should be subject to the principle of 'minimalism' – the images of violence or depicted violence should not be more graphic than was needed to establish the story.

This qualitative research was followed by a quantitative stage, administered by Market and Opinion Research International Ltd (MORI). A questionnaire was designed, following extensive piloting, which addressed the issues described. In particular, it considered the viewer's relationship with violent material in factual programming and tested the hypotheses derived from the editing process. In addition to these data gathered from 1,296 adults, a sub-sample of 260 video owners were shown three short clips from transmitted factual programmes. Satellite owners, with access to 24 hour news coverage and a variety of additional reconstruction and fly-on-the-wall programmes, formed part of a boosted sample.

The Review presents the results of the different elements of the research, moving from a general overview of the results to the specific details of the editing groups. Trend data are described briefly and the Review ends with a collection of essays from those who work in, or take an interest in, the broadcast of the factual programme.

# RESEARCH

# 1. The Survey Findings

## Introduction

This Section principally reports on the findings of the quantitative study conducted by MORI and also refers to the qualitative research conducted through the editing groups. Section 2 recounts the detail of the editing groups themselves.

## *Violence in society*

> *'I think it's frightening because it's commonplace now as though we're expecting it; it's become the norm. It's the most frightening thing. How has it become normal to be like this?'*
> (Woman, 55+ years old)

> *'If there is any young men walking towards me and they look a bit strange, I'm frightened. I stand back and let them get past.'*
> (Woman, 40–55 years old)

These comments, like others in this section, were made by people who took part in the editing groups (reported on fully in Section 2), and represented a genuine feeling of vulnerability particularly noticeable in women and among older people in general. The quantitative research therefore sought to investigate how exposed respondents felt to violence based on the measures they took to decrease their vulnerability. That is, how many precautions they took to try to ensure security for themselves and their families.

Most respondents claimed to take some of the steps listed to reduce the risk to themselves or their family. While the presence of children in the household did not seem to be a key discriminant (and it could have been supposed that it might be), gender was. Women were particularly likely to take measures to reduce personal risk. They avoided going out after dark and sat in crowded carriages in trains and buses. There was an indication that men, on the other hand, would take precautions which would enable them to use their own strength to remove themselves from unpleasant situations. As one might expect, age was a factor too. Younger respondents were less likely to take many of the measures described, while older respondents, on the whole, showed a similar pattern to the female respondents, although not always as dramatically. A summary of the measures taken based on age and gender is given in the following table.

### Table 1. Measures taken for personal security

|  | Total sample | Male | Female | Households with children |
|---|---|---|---|---|
| Base | 100% | 48% | 52% | 37% |
|  | % | % | % | % |
| Lock all doors and windows whenever you leave the house/flat | 94 | 93 | 95 | 93 |
| Not carry valuables where they can be seen | 51 | 46 | 56 | 48 |
| Lock doors when when you are in the house/flat | 46 | 40 | 51 | 38 |
| Choose a safe route | 44 | 31 | 55 | 47 |
| Do not open door until person identified | 43 | 32 | 53 | 39 |
| Avoid going out after dark on your own | 34 | 12 | 55 | 34 |
| Lock your car doors when you are driving | 33 | 26 | 38 | 33 |
| Check regularly whether anyone is following you | 29 | 19 | 39 | 34 |
| Sit in crowded part of train or bus | 27 | 12 | 41 | 28 |
| Avoid passing close to unlit doorways | 27 | 14 | 40 | 30 |
| Tell your children not to go out or stay out late on their own | 27 | 25 | 29 | 55 |
| Wear flat/practical shoes | 26 | 18 | 33 | 19 |
| Use a burglar alarm or triggered lighting | 24 | 24 | 24 | 21 |
| Belong to a neighbourhood watch scheme | 22 | 20 | 24 | 22 |
| Keep a dog | 22 | 20 | 24 | 23 |
| Take a weapon to bed at night | 6 | 6 | 5 | 6 |
| Carry object which you could use for defence | 6 | 6 | 5 | 6 |
| Go to self-defence classes | 4 | 5 | 2 | 5 |
| Carry a personal alarm | 4 | 1 | 6 | 3 |
| Other | 3 | 3 | 4 | 2 |
| None of these | 1 | 1 | – | 1 |
| 1–5 measures taken | 51 | 67 | 36 | 49 |
| 6–10 measures taken | 41 | 29 | 51 | 41 |
| 11+ measures taken | 8 | 2 | 13 | 9 |

Unless otherwise specified, all tabular data presented in this Review are based on a nationally representative survey conducted for the Broadcasting Standards Council by MORI in September 1993. All data are based on a total sample of 1,296 adults.
Unless otherwise specified, 'don't know' answers are excluded.

**Table 2. Measures taken for personal security – variables of gender and age**

|  | 1–5 measures % | 6–10 measures % | 11+ measures % |
|---|---|---|---|
| Total | 51 | 41 | 8 |
| *Male* |  |  |  |
| 18–24 | 71 | 22 | 5 |
| 25–34 | 68 | 28 | 3 |
| 35–44 | 68 | 29 | 3 |
| 45–54 | 64 | 34 | 1 |
| 55–64 | 65 | 33 | 1 |
| 65+ | 62 | 34 | 3 |
| *Female* |  |  |  |
| 18–24 | 41 | 44 | 16 |
| 25–34 | 32 | 55 | 12 |
| 35–44 | 29 | 54 | 8 |
| 45–54 | 33 | 57 | 10 |
| 55–64 | 33 | 51 | 16 |
| 65+ | 39 | 51 | 9 |

## Knowledge of personal violence

A further set of questions asked respondents about their exposure to violence, either directly or indirectly. It was of interest to know if this coloured their attitudes to violence on television.

Experience of violence against property, including knowing someone who had experienced a burglary, ranked fairly high (mentioned by about half the sample). Men, however, were far more likely to have known about, or been involved in, physical acts of violence (such as fights, physical attacks etc). This was true particularly of younger men.

However, it was the younger male respondents who were most robust in their attitudes to violence on television. It would seem that the sense of vulnerability noted above, driven by gender and age, had greater influence on attitudes towards televisual violence, even in factual programming, than the experience of actual violence. Results from the editing groups, which formed the study's qualitative research, confirmed this quantified finding (see next section).

## Attitudes to violence on television

The Annual Review has always examined respondents' attitudes to the three key areas within the Council's remit – the portrayal of violence, the depiction of sexual activity and the use of bad language. A full account of this year's findings for the depiction of sexual activity and bad language, and an account of the trends to be noted, can be found in Section 3. Table 3 shows respondents' attitudes to the level of violence they perceived to be on television. It can be seen that two-thirds of respondents thought that there was 'too much' violence on television, which was a significantly higher proportion than those who thought that there was either 'too much' bad language (57 per cent) or 'too much' sexual activity (40 per cent) portrayed.

### Table 3. Levels of violence on television

|            | %  |
|------------|----|
| Too much   | 66 |
| About right| 32 |
| Too little | 2  |

Demographically-distinct groups of respondents accounted for significant proportions of each response group. Women (74 per cent), those aged over 45 (81 per cent), and those belonging to the socio-economic groups AB[1] (71 per cent) were significantly more likely to say that there was 'too much' violence on television in comparison with the sample as a whole (66 per cent).

Men were slightly more likely (40 per cent of men compared with 32 per cent of the sample as a whole) to say that the level of violence on television was 'about right', as were satellite viewers (37 per cent) and those with children (38 per cent). Younger respondents, those aged under 34, also were significantly more likely (49 per cent) to agree with this statement.

Violence was the issue mentioned by a significant number of respondents (55 per cent) as causing them the most concern when considering each of the three areas.

### Viewing factual programmes

It was important to understand the role that factual programmes played in people's lives before asking questions about their attitudes towards these. It was also necessary to establish knowledge of the genres under consideration in order to understand .ne responses. It was of interest as well to know if there were particular attitudes held by those who were avid consumers of, say, news and current affairs or of reconstruction programmes.

Early in the quantitative research, questions were asked about the extent people watched each of the programme genres being considered. What was found was an almost universal viewing of the news – 95 per cent of the sample watched the news sometimes and 85 per cent watched it at least once a day. Indeed, one-third of the sample claimed to watch the news on television twice a day or more and, in the over 65 year olds, this increased to 52 per cent of that group.

While almost every one of the respondents seemed to watch the news, significant numbers also watched reconstruction programmes and documentaries. Over four-fifths of the sample said they watched each of these types of programme. About half said they watched reconstructions at least once a week (and nearly one in five said they watched more than that). In comparison, viewing of documentaries was mar-

---

1   For a definition of socio-economic groups, see Appendix 3.

ginally less frequent overall, with 42 per cent saying they watched them about once a week, although nearly one-third of the sample said they watched them more frequently than that.

Over two-thirds of the sample said that they watched all three genres of factual programming.

Although those who watched television news showed little demographic variation because the levels of viewing were so high (particularly among the over 65 year olds), viewing of reconstruction programmes and documentaries did show some diversity. Those who watched reconstructions were more likely to be female, aged between 35 and 44, and of the socio-economic group D. There were also more of this group among satellite viewers. In comparison, those who watched documentaries were likely to be older (45+) and of the socio-economic groups ABC1.

Those with access to satellite television were asked if they watched the news, reconstruction programmes or documentaries on satellite channels. Around two in five said that they did so in addition to watching the same genres on terrestrial television.

## Attitudes to children and the news

Respondents were asked a series of questions about the Watershed at 9.00 pm, the time at which parents are expected to take increased responsibility for the programmes their children watch (see Section 3). In particular, the sample was asked if they thought that there was a Watershed for the news, and then, whether they thought one would be appropriate. As Table 4 shows, most respondents (including those without children at home) felt that there was no Watershed for the news, although, in fact, there is. However, opinions were split over whether there should be one; with a significant proportion of respondents thinking that there should.

### Table 4. News and the Watershed

|  | Total sample | Homes with children |
|---|---|---|
| Base | 100% | 37% |
|  | % | % |
| **Is there a Watershed for the news?** |  |  |
| Yes | 14 | 13 |
| No | 69 | 75 |
| Don't know | 17 | 12 |
| **Should there be a Watershed for the news?** |  |  |
| Yes | 40 | 43 |
| No | 52 | 51 |
| Don't know | 8 | 6 |

This seemed to show some desire to protect children, not just from unsuitable fiction but from unpleasant reality as well. Research into other areas, such as the depiction of sexual activity, would support this – parents expressed a wish to preserve their children's 'innocence' for as long as possible, and television was felt (at times) to raise issues they would prefer not to address at a particular stage (*Sex and Sexuality in Broadcasting*, BSC Annual Review 1992). It would seem that this was true also of violent images in real life, as represented on television.

Respondents were asked whether or not they had viewed television with children recently and if they had felt obliged to turn off or change channels because something was shown which they thought to be unacceptable (for full results see Section 3). Of those respondents who had children at home, nearly half – 46 per cent – had done this. Their reasons, in ranked order, were the portrayal of violence, sex and bad language. Of those who had taken such action, 16 per cent had switched off documentaries and two in five of them said it was because of violent material. Thirteen per cent said they had switched off the news and nearly half gave their reasons as violence.

In further support of the suggestion that some respondents wished, at times, to shield children from unpleasant images, was the finding that nearly two-thirds of the sample (62 per cent) said that they felt less comfortable when watching factual programmes with children present, while a third said it made no difference. The majority, over 80 per cent, said that it did not matter which genre of factual programming was under consideration. When asked how they dealt with this discomfort, most (69 per cent) said they would turn the television off or change channels. Thirty per cent said they would try and discuss the issues raised, answer questions, seek to reassure the children while 15 per cent said they would send the children out of the room. The remainder mainly said they would seek to draw their children's attention away from the television.

### Attitudes to factual programming

In his essay, John Wilson, former BBC Controller, Editorial Policy, says that it is incumbent upon factual television to be 'more restrained' in the violence it shows as it deals mainly in the aftermath of violence rather than in acts of violence, as fiction does. The Council was particularly interested to establish if respondents considered that violence in factual programming was different from violence in fiction.

As Table 5 shows, opinions were reasonably evenly divided – violence is violence, regardless of its source. Those who had taken a large number of precautions for their personal security and those with children were marginally more likely than the sample as a whole to say that the violence in a factual programme was greater in impact than similar violence depicted in a piece of fiction.

**Table 5. Would the same action seem more or less violent if it were a factual programme than if it were fiction?**

|  | % |
| --- | --- |
| More | 39 |
| Less | 26 |
| No difference | 34 |

*'Even though no matter how realistically any kind of acting is done, you always know it's fiction, there is always something that tells you that it's fictional and it acts as a kind of barrier.'*
(Man, 40–45 years old)

Respondents were asked to comment on the way in which their attitudes to violence on television might have affected their behaviour – see Table 6. (Some of the behavioural characteristics of respondents in terms of the measures they took to protect themselves from violence have already been noted.)

**Table 6. Attitudes to violence on television and effects on behaviour**

| | Strongly agree % | Tend to agree % | Neither % | Tend to disagree % | Strongly disagree % |
|---|---|---|---|---|---|
| Violence on TV simply reflects the state of society | 24 | 51 | 6 | 14 | 4 |
| Violence in factual TV makes people *more* ready to accept violence in real life | 17 | 41 | 10 | 23 | 8 |
| Watching violence in factual programmes has made me behave much more carefully | 21 | 46 | 14 | 14 | 4 |
| Violence on TV has made people *unnecessarily* afraid | 13 | 43 | 11 | 27 | 6 |

Three-quarters of the sample said they felt that violence on television reflected the state of the society in which they lived. As has been noted on other occasions and will be seen in the more detailed analysis of the editing groups, violence in the 'real world' was seen to be reflected by television, particularly by those people who felt themselves to be vulnerable. Women and older respondents were more likely to agree with this statement, as were those from the socio-economic group, C2. Those with children living at home were slightly more likely to disagree, which could be a reflection of the fact that they belonged to a younger age group and younger respondents, in general, were less likely to feel threatened by violence. In response to the statement 'Violence in factual television makes people more ready to accept violence in real life', 58 per cent of the sample said that they agreed. Again there was a feeling that increased exposure to violence on television, particularly as a reflection of reality, created a feeling that violence was now more prevalent. Respondents aged over 65, and those from the socio-economic group, C2, were more likely to agree with this statement.

The third statement, 'Watching violence in factual programmes has made me behave more carefully', sought to understand to what extent behaviour was altered by real violence, brought into the home through the television screen, rather than by personal experience. Two-thirds of the sample agreed with this statement. Those groups who might consider themselves vulnerable, in the light of their own physical limitations, agreed with this more strongly. For example, women were nearly 25 per cent more likely to agree strongly with this than the sample as a whole (and three-quarters as likely as men). Similarly those aged 65+ were over a third more likely to agree strongly and those who took particular precautions over their physical security also fell into this category.

The final statement asked if respondents thought violence on television had made people unnecessarily afraid – about half felt it had, while a third disagreed. Those who disagreed were more likely to be women, while older respondents (those aged 45 and above) agreed that the fear may be unnecessary.

So while exposure to violence in factual programming, and the feeling that it reflected a more violent society, created a tension, many respondents (particularly those who felt themselves to be more exposed to violence) seemed resigned to it. They might accept their fear was not warranted, but it existed nonetheless.

Respondents had been asked if they thought that the same violent action would seem more or less violent if it were in a factual programme than if it were in fiction (see Table 5 above). Responses had been equally divided between those who said that factual violence would seem more violent and those who had said that it would make no difference – violence was violence. Respondents were now asked *why* they felt differently about violence in the two types of programming. Of those who said they felt differently about factual programming, over one-third said it was because the programmes were an account of reality. More than a quarter of this group also said that violence in fiction could be avoided and was not necessary, while nearly the same number said that fictional violence was exaggerated.

In order to see whether this recognition of violence in factual programmes as being necessary and inevitable was affected by the particular programme type being viewed, respondents were asked to consider whether violence in the news, specifically, was more acceptable than violence in other programmes. Over half the sample (55 per cent) said that it was. When asked the same question about violence portrayed in reconstruction programmes, this fell to 43 per cent, and a similar response was obtained for documentaries (41 per cent said violence in this genre was more acceptable than in other programmes). In each of these two cases, just under 40 per cent of respondents also said that the genre (reconstruction or documentary) made no difference to the acceptability of the violence shown. It may be surmised then, that if violence was to be shown, the news was the most acceptable of the programme genres for it. Bearing in mind these results and the findings from the editing groups, the news – rooted as it is in real life – was allowed greatest licence in the material it could show. (Richard Wald, in his essay, also suggests that the difference between the news and documentaries is that, in a news bulletin, any violence 'is over in a short while' while in a documentary – because of its length and the depth in which it can analyse a subject – 'the power of violence is magnified tenfold').

This study also sought to find out if the time at which a factual programme was scheduled affected the acceptability of violent images. As Table 7 shows, about half the respondents were fairly clear that such material should be shown, regardless of the genre, because the violence was real, but that it should be shown at a later time than it currently was. The remainder of the sample was split between those who said violent content could be shown at any time and those who said it should be edited out.

**Table 7. Violence in factual programming and scheduling**

|  | News and Current Affairs % | Reconstruction % | Documentaries % |
|---|---|---|---|
| Anytime | 29 | 21 | 23 |
| Later | 50 | 58 | 55 |
| Edited | 21 | 22 | 22 |

This seems to indicate that the editing-out of violence in the news and other factual programming prior to the Watershed would be welcomed by these respondents, while a news bulletin with fewer restrictions placed upon it would be acceptable after 9.00 pm.

In order to investigate further the hypothesis that the news, in particular, and factual programmes in general, had fewer conditions placed upon them than other programmes, respondents were asked how they approached violent material in the different genres. They were first asked if they thought sufficient warning was given about such content in the news (see Table 8). Nearly two-thirds (63 per cent) said they thought so, but a significant minority (35 per cent) said there was not enough. Those from the socio-economic groups DE felt most strongly that insufficient warning was given (43 per cent said this compared with 35 per cent across the sample as a whole) and also those with children in the home (39 per cent).

Similar responses were made when respondents were asked to consider reconstruction programmes, with 69 per cent saying enough warning was given and 30 per cent saying there was not enough. Again those in the socio-economic group E were more likely to say there was not enough warning given.

When considering documentaries, 66 per cent of respondents said that there was enough warning given while 33 per cent disagreed.

These three genres were compared with fiction to test the perceived difference between factual and fictional violence. Most respondents (63 per cent) felt there was not enough warning given about violence in fictional programmes. This is to be contrasted with factual programmes, considered by the majority of respondents to provide adequate notice of material to be transmitted.

**Table 8. Warnings given for violent material in each programme type**

|  | Enough warning % | Not enough warning % | Too much warning % |
|---|---|---|---|
| News and current affairs | 63 | 35 | 1 |
| Reconstruction | 69 | 30 | * |
| Documentaries | 66 | 33 | * |
| Fiction | 36 | 63 | 1 |

Despite this finding that most respondents in the quantitative study felt there was sufficient warning given about the violence that might be seen in the news, some respondents in the editing groups had expressed a concern, saying that they could not be adequately prepared for the range of material they might see.

> (Re. untransmitted footage from Bosnia) *'The news is something you switch on and have to watch what you are given, but if it was a documentary, I think yes (such material would be acceptable).'*
> (Woman, 25–34 years old)

To test this difference in response to the news in comparison with documentaries, respondents in the quantitative survey were questioned about the additional steps they took to protect themselves from material they may not wish to see in reconstruction programmes and documentaries. Over half of the sample (57 per cent) said that they checked the subject matter of these programmes before switching on, while 41 per cent said they just switched on and watched. Women and older respondents were more likely to check first, as were those in the groups AB and E. The younger respondents and men were less likely to check first, but switched the programme straight on.

In order to gauge the level of offence, if any, violent material in factual programmes might cause, respondents were asked if they had ever turned the television off, changed channels or walked out of a room because they were personally disgusted by an item on television. Twenty eight per cent of respondents said that they had. (For the full results to this question, see Section 3.) Of this group, 25 per cent had turned off because they were disgusted by the violence portrayed. When probed about the programme in which the violence had occurred, about one-quarter (27 per cent) said it had been in a film, while 22 per cent had turned off or away from the news. Plays (13 per cent) and documentaries (10 per cent) were the next most cited programme genres. So, while violence in factual programmes might be more acceptable, it was as likely to disgust as violence in fiction.

To explore the above finding further, respondents were asked if they felt more comfortable, or less, if they watched violent material in factual programmes on their own. The majority, 76 per cent, said it made no difference to how comfortable they felt.

A far smaller group, 14 per cent, said they felt less comfortable when watching alone. But when particular groups of respondents were considered, such as women, the proportions saying they felt less comfortable changed. Twenty-three per cent of women said they felt less comfortable watching alone. Also, as might be expected, those who took most care to protect themselves (11+ measures taken for personal security) were more likely to say that they felt less comfortable (27 per cent).

The principal reason given by these respondents was that factual violence increased their feelings of isolation when they were alone. They felt more frightened because the violence was real and they felt that it could happen to them (see Table 9). More than one in ten respondents also mentioned that they had no-one with whom to share their discomfort. Some of the older female respondents in the editing groups had referred also to this 'internalization' of their discomfort and fear when watching actual violence.

> 'When you are on your own you don't have anyone to discuss it with and so you take it in and worry about it.'
> (Woman, 55+ years old)

**Table 9. Why do you feel less comfortable watching factual violence on your own?**

|  | Total sample | Men | Women | 11+ measures |
|---|---|---|---|---|
| Base/total sample | 14% |  |  |  |
| Base/responding to question | 100% | 15% | 84% | 15% |
|  | % | % | % | % |
| Feeling of isolation/feel more vulnerable | 31 | 32 | 31 | 30 |
| Feel more frightened | 24 | 25 | 24 | 22 |
| Nervous/imagination runs away with me | 19 | 18 | 19 | 18 |
| Feel it could happen to me/ reality of it | 16 | 25 | 14 | 18 |
| No-one to discuss it with/ share feelings with | 14 | 14 | 14 | 11 |
| Don't like it/switch it off | 8 | 4 | 9 | 11 |

A more detailed analysis of the results shows that gender was more important as a discriminatory variable in this context than age. Nonetheless the combination of age and gender increased the sense of isolation and vulnerability.

Further, the more precautions that respondents took for their personal security, the more likely they were to say they felt frightened or nervous when viewing alone.

Of those who had said they felt more comfortable watching violent scenes in factual programmes on their own, 32 per cent said this was because they felt they could deal with things better on their own, while 26 per cent said it meant that they did not have to worry about the reactions of those watching with them. Men particularly were more likely to mention the latter reason (31 per cent).

Most respondents (three quarters) said that it made no difference to their responses to the above questions if they were watching the news, a reconstruction programme or a documentary.

As has already been seen, just over 20 per cent of the sample said they had turned away from the news because they were personally disgusted by something they had seen. The entire sample was now asked what they would do if they were watching the news and a violent item, which they found particularly unpleasant, came on. As Table 10 shows, over half the sample (56 per cent) said they would keep watching.

Most of the remainder (45 per cent of the sample) took avoiding action such as switching channels, switching the television off, or looking away.

**Table 10. Action taken if violent item on news**

|  | % |
| --- | --- |
| Keep watching | 56 |
| Look away | 20 |
| Switch channels | 9 |
| Switch off | 8 |
| Stop watching | 8 |
| Turn sound down | * |

Men were significantly more likely to say they would keep watching (71 per cent of men compared with 56 per cent of the sample as a whole) as were those in the younger age groups and those belonging to the socio-economic group, D. Satellite viewers and those who said there was 'too little' or 'about the right amount' of violence on television were also more likely to be in this group.

When asked why they kept watching (Table 11), the reason cited by most of this sample (94 per cent) was that they believed they had a duty to watch ('I think we have a duty to keep ourselves informed, even if it is sometimes unpleasant'). This sense of duty was further amplified in the editing groups. Respondents throughout the survey, by and large, were of the view that if an event had happened and it was newsworthy, it should be reported – however violent. Equally they felt they should stay and watch it so that they were informed. It was believed that the news would not sensationalize events, although there was the feeling (already reported) that children should be protected from the worst of the visual images.

Over three-quarters of the sample said they would keep watching because they watched their 'regular' programmes and occasional violent scenes would not deter them. Duty and habit then, were the prime reasons mentioned for carrying on viewing. While those expressing the former reason were not demographically distinct, those who gave the latter reason (watching was a matter of habit) were significantly more likely to be from the group, C2.

Over half the sample also said they kept watching because violence on factual television did not upset[1] them seriously enough. They showed an acceptance of the violence, and were significantly more likely to be male (62 per cent compared with 54 per cent across the total sample) and young (61 per cent of 18–24 year olds). There was a slight bias as well among those from the socio-economic groups, C2D, with 59 per cent of them saying that the violence did not upset them seriously enough. Those who felt the level of violence on television was 'about right' or that there was 'too little' on television were also likely to agree.

Forty per cent of respondents said that once they were sitting down and watching

---

1   The use of the word 'upset' was derived from the research conducted in the editing groups and appeared to describe the emotions respondents felt most adequately.

something, they were not inclined to change channels even if an upsetting violent scene appeared, while nearly one-third of the sample (31 per cent) admitted that violence could be exciting to watch. This last group tended to be younger (under 34 years old), male and more likely to belong to the group of respondents who felt that the amount of violence on television was 'about right' or 'too little'.

Just over a quarter of these respondents who currently kept watching said that they felt, if the violence continued at its present level, they would have to stop watching their regular factual programmes. Age was a strong discriminator here with 43 per cent of those aged over 65 agreeing with this in comparison with 26 per cent of the sample as a whole. Women were also inclined to agree that they felt they might have to stop watching their normal programmes.

**Table 11. Why do you keep watching a factual programme with violence that is upsetting?**

|  |  |
|---|---:|
| Base/total sample | 56% |
| Base/responding to question | 100% |
|  | % |
| I think we have a duty to keep ourselves informed, even if it is sometimes unpleasant | 94 |
| I always watch my regular programmes, and occasional violent scenes won't stop me | 78 |
| I'm not seriously enough upset by violence on TV | 54 |
| Once I've sat down comfortably I prefer to stay put | 41 |
| Sometimes violence is exciting to watch | 31 |
| I have always watched them, but if the violence keeps on at its present level I'll have to change | 26 |
| None apply | 1 |
| Don't know | * |

As we have seen, under half the sample said they took action to avoid material with upsetting violent images (of those who said this, 70 per cent were women). Nearly half of those who avoided such material said they were most likely simply to look away.

Respondents were asked why they stopped watching (see Table 12). The most-often cited reasons for turning away from the violence were that it was 'real' and not fictional, and that respondents did not feel that they needed to see pictures to know the event had happened. (This finding was mirrored in the editing group research.) Half of this sample said that they felt really upset by violence in factual programmes and nearly the same number said that, although they appreciated they had a duty to watch such material (because it was factual and real), they could not bear to do so. It is interesting to note that over one-third said that they were bored with all the violence they saw, suggesting that it had lost its impact.

Table 12. Why do you stop watching a factual programme with violence that is upsetting?

| | |
|---|---|
| Base/total sample | 45% |
| Base/responding to question | 100% |
| | % |
| I know the violence has really happened | 75 |
| I do not have to keep seeing violence to know what is happening | 73 |
| I feel really upset by all violence on TV | 50 |
| Although we have a duty to keep ourselves informed, I personally cannot face it | 45 |
| There is so much violence on TV so that I am bored by it | 36 |
| None apply | 1 |
| Don't know | 14 |

As already noted, women formed the largest proportion of this group, and so were more likely to agree with all the statements, but the last one, referring to boredom. Men were more likely to agree that they took avoiding action because they were bored. Those in the 18–24 age bracket and those aged over 65 were also more likely to say this than the sample as a whole.

## Testing hypotheses derived from the editing groups

Following the editing groups certain hypotheses governing viewers' responses to violence in factual programming were posed. These have already been mentioned in the introduction and the detail of the way in which they were arrived at is described in the following section. However, the quantitative research set out, as one of its principal tasks, to consider each hypothesis and to try and understand how far they might be deemed to be 'principles'. A brief description of each is given below, and the questions which sought to test it are also mentioned.

### Hypothesis 1: The principle of 'closeness'

> (Re. footage from Vietnam) *'These pictures would disturb rather than create fear. There's a big difference there – it's something that is at a distance rather than a crime which could happen to you, and for that reason having pictures of war on television seems to be more acceptable.'*
> (Male satellite viewers)

This hypothesis stated that the more a respondent or viewer could relate to a scene of violence in factual programming, the more disturbing it became. 'Distant' violence was less disturbing. This distance may be geographical or time-related (such as the Vietnam War) or it could be related to lifestyle or how fantastical the episode or scene was. Other research conducted into television fiction would support this; respondents found violence in costume drama easier to accept than violence in a contemporary drama with a backdrop to which they could relate (*Violence in Television Fiction, BSC Annual Review 1990*).

It has already been seen that many respondents considered 'real' violence to be more upsetting than fictional violence, even though they expected to see the former, or felt that they should. To test the hypothesis of 'closeness' further, the questionnaire asked respondents if they would be more or less upset if the violence in a factual programme involved people who were like their friends and neighbours. An overwhelming majority (82 per cent) of the sample said 'yes' – they could now identify with the violence and bring it within their realm of experience. Women especially said they would be more upset, as did those aged under 34, and those from the socio-economic groups C2D.

Similarly respondents who had a special interest in the subject matter of a particular programme (for example, a documentary) were split between those who said they would find the violence in that programme more upsetting and those who said it would make no difference. The results of the editing groups showed that such subject matter could be the hunt for a local killer, or other local violence, for example, bringing the violence closer to home.

Respondents were also asked if they would be more or less upset if the violence was happening in another country. As the Table below shows, the majority said it would make no difference, although a significant number (30 per cent) said that they would be less upset. Again, geographical closeness and the ability to identify with the context of the violence increased respondents' involvement with the violent images.

### Table 13. Testing the principle of 'closeness'

|  | More upset % | Less upset % | No difference % |
|---|---|---|---|
| The victim is someone like your own friends and neighbours | 82 | 1 | 17 |
| The programme is of special interest to you | 43 | 12 | 45 |
| It is happening in another country | 17 | 30 | 53 |

The principle of closeness then would seem to be appropriate. This was particularly true if the factual programme contained an element of dramatization (such as a programme using reconstructions) and the characters portrayed were made recognizable and familiar to the viewer. Recognition of place and identification with the individuals in the event portrayed were also prime variables. This is illustrated more clearly in the next section.

*Hypothesis 2: The principle of 'certainty'*

The second hypothesis was the principle of certainty which stated that an act of violence would shock less if the viewer understood what was happening, or if they knew beforehand what the outcome of the scene would be.

This was tested in the quantitative research through two statements. The first asked respondents if they would be more, or less, upset if they knew beforehand what was going to happen. As Table 14 shows, respondents were equally divided between those who said they would be less upset and those who said it would make no difference. A small group said that it would make them more upset. A further question was asked which examined the frequency with which a scene might be repeated, 'Would you be more/less upset if you have seen it often already?' Again, respondents were quite equally divided between those who said that they would be less upset and those who said that it made no difference.

While there were no key demographic differences between the respondent groups to the former statement (other than a slight bias towards those aged under 24 agreeing they would be 'less upset' if they knew what was going to happen beforehand), there were more marked differences for the latter statement. Those from the socio-economic groups AB were significantly more likely to say that repeated viewings of an item would lead them to become less upset, while male respondents and those aged under 44 were also inclined to agree with this statement.

Foreknowledge seemed to help respondents cope better with a scene of violence in a factual programme. So a news report which told the viewer how the conflict or violence they were about to see ended, for example, prior to the footage being shown, would remove some of the ensuing discomfort by removing doubt.

**Table 14. Testing the principle of 'certainty'**

|  | More upset % | Less upset % | No difference % |
|---|---|---|---|
| You are told beforehand what is going to happen | 8 | 44 | 48 |
| You have seen it often already | 10 | 41 | 49 |

(Re. clip from *World in Action*) '*It was best to keep that in to let you know he got away. It could have been a dead body, we should have been told before we saw the actual crash. Looking at that it looks as though they had drowned him and then suddenly you see something coming through the glass window. You automatically thought that they had drowned him.*'
(Women, 40–55 years old)

*Hypothesis 3: The principle of 'status'*

The third hypothesis posited as a result of the editing groups research, was the principle of status which said that the greater the sympathy the viewer had with the victim, the greater the disturbance to the viewer. This principle also stated that if the victim was seen to have a low claim to be regarded justly, a higher level of violent imagery was tolerated.

The questionnaire tested this in a variety of ways (see Table 15). Respondents were asked how upset they would be if the victim was weak or vulnerable. An overwhelming majority (87 per cent) said that they would be more upset whereas, if they did not know much about the victim, respondents felt that their reactions to the scene would be unaffected. A significant minority (27 per cent) said that they would be less upset.

If the respondents felt that the victim deserved to be punished – even though the violence seen was considered upsetting – or if they thought the victim was partly to blame for the act, they were likely to say that they would be less upset or that it would make no difference to their reaction to the violence. This was especially true of male respondents. Age also made a difference and the younger respondents, particularly those aged under 34, responded in a less tolerant way if the victim was felt to be at fault in any way. These findings based on demographic characteristics are further amplified by the results from the editing groups.

The degree to which the viewer empathized with the victim then, was of great importance to the strength of reaction to a particular scene, even in factual television.

### Table 15. Testing the principle of 'status'

|  | More upset % | Less upset % | No difference % |
|---|---|---|---|
| The victim is particularly weak and vulnerable | 87 | 2 | 11 |
| You are not told much about the victim | 17 | 27 | 55 |
| The victim deserves to be punished | 12 | 45 | 43 |
| The victim is partly to blame | 9 | 40 | 51 |

*Hypothesis 4. The principle of 'minimalism'*

This hypothesis said that the images of violence within a factual programme, be they depiction or actuality, should not go into greater detail than was necessary to illustrate the point being made, or story being told.

> (Re. clip from local news item) *'We know what he's done so we don't want all the details – it's unnecessary detail. We don't need to have all the sound effects (reference to 'ripping ear') of the fight. The jury might have to sit and listen to it all but it's not necessary for us to. We just need to know the verdict. There is just too much of what you don't need to know. We have our own imagination to put pictures to the words.'* (Women, 16–24 years old)

The quantitative research tested the hypothesis of minimalism by examining respondents' attitudes to violent images in factual programmes on the basis that they explained the event, and also on a 'need to know' criterion, which was often a reason given for the tolerance of violent content in factual programmes.

Although respondents were told that the violent scenes were necessary to make it clear what really happened, this was not felt to be enough justification. A significant proportion of the sample – over one-third – said they would be more upset. About one-half said it would make no difference to how upset they would feel. Once again the dilemma respondents faced became apparent – they accepted that violence in factual material was reality and therefore had a place on their screens but they were, or could be, upset by it. Similarly even though it was important for the public to know the facts of the violence, most respondents said that it would not affect how upset they would be, while a quarter of them said they would be more upset. (See also the essay by John Simpson regarding the Chatila massacre, the aftermath of which he witnessed.) Respondents agreed therefore that the minimum of violence in such programming was most acceptable.

### Table 16. Testing the principle of 'minimalism'

|  | More upset % | Less upset % | No difference % |
|---|---|---|---|
| The violence is necessary to make it really clear what happened | 37 | 15 | 48 |
| It is really important for the public to know the facts | 25 | 16 | 59 |

Related to this principle was an hypothesis which stated that the more production values were added into an item featuring violence in factual programming, such as reconstructions, the greater the upset caused to the viewer. This was also tested against the sample in the quantitative stage of the research.

### Table 17. Testing the importance of production values

|  | More upset % | Less upset % | No difference % |
|---|---|---|---|
| The music increases the dramatic effect | 58 | 4 | 37 |
| The reporter sounds genuinely upset about the violence | 63 | 5 | 32 |
| The sounds are edited out | 11 | 36 | 52 |
| The violence is shown in a completely realistic way | 45 | 8 | 46 |

The use of dramatic devices such as music, or the heightened emotion of the 'objective' reporter, all influenced how strongly the respondents thought they would react to the scene in question. Women were more responsive to the use of these production techniques, being more likely to agree that music or an emotional report would make them more upset.

Editing out the sounds would, for many respondents, decrease the level of upset they might feel with the violence they were viewing. If a reconstruction were made to look completely realistic so that the audience was totally engaged in the action depicted, then the respondents were split between those who thought they would be more upset and those who thought it would make no difference. Women in particular thought that they would be more upset by the realism. The more real or engaging the action, the more upsetting it was then, to many respondents.

### Responses to video clips – the quantitative results

A subsample of 260 respondents were shown a set of three video clips, illustrating each of the three genres that were under consideration in this quantitative study. Having established whether or not respondents had seen the programme which contained the clip, they were asked how upset they had been by it, and their reasons for their response. They were also asked to consider how differently they might feel if the clip belonged to a different genre.

### Reconstruction – World in Action

The first clip was one used in the editing groups' project and was a reconstruction taken from a documentary broadcast between 8.30 pm and 9.00 pm. (For full details of the clip shown see Section 2.) Only 8 per cent of respondents in this sample had seen the programme, from which the clip was taken, when it was broadcast.

All respondents were shown the clip and asked how upset they had been by it (see Table 18). Most respondents were upset by it to some extent, but women and the older respondents in particular were likely to say that they were 'very upset' (50 per cent of women and 69 per cent of those aged 65+ said this in comparison with 39 per cent of the total sample).

Nearly one in five respondents said that they were upset by the clip because of the fact that 'someone could do that to another human being'. Men were slightly more likely to say this than women. Women were more likely to mention reasons related to the report itself – 15 per cent of the sample said they were upset because of the detail given in the description of what happened, while 18 per cent of women said this.

#### Table 18. Reactions to the reconstruction clip

|  | % |
| --- | --- |
| Very upset | 39 |
| Slightly upset | 33 |
| Not at all | 25 |
| Don't know | 3 |

All tabular data presented in this section are based on a subsample of 260 video owners derived from the nationally representative sample of 1,296 adults, recruited for the Broadcasting Standards Council by MORI in September 1993.

### News bulletin – Bosnia

The second clip that respondents were shown was transmitted in news bulletins, and was a report from Bosnia. This clip was also used in the editing groups and for a full description, refer to Section 2.

Again most respondents said that they had been upset by it, although more now said that they were 'slightly upset' in comparison with the reconstruction clip shown. This could be a result of some of the findings already noted – the Bosnian conflict, being a war and happening in another country, was divorced from the principle of closeness on two counts. Further, images from Bosnia had been on television frequently at the time of this research and there might have been some of the ennui with the repeated images of violence that some respondents had mentioned before.

**Table 19. Reactions to the news bulletin clip**

|  | % |
| --- | --- |
| Very upset | 32 |
| Slightly upset | 42 |
| Not at all | 23 |
| Don't know | 3 |

When respondents were asked why they had found the clip upsetting, about a quarter mentioned the fact that they saw dead bodies. 14 per cent said they found the fact that the violence was real particularly upsetting, while nearly the same number referred to the detail of the report such as the cutting off of victims' hands and heads. Again, women were more likely to mention the detail of the reports as having made them more upset.

*Documentary* – Testimonies

The final clip that was shown to respondents had not been available at the time the editing groups were conducted. It was taken from a documentary called *Testimonies* which had been broadcast at 9.00 pm. The chosen extract first shows part of an interview with the soldier who had filmed the arrest of a suspect. He explains that he had thought that, by filming the event, he could stop the violence. His film is then shown. In it, a young man is stopped and arrested violently. Among the incidents seen is one in which his fingers are repeatedly hit with a gun while he tries to hold on to some rails. A woman pleads for him. (The film was shot in Israel and showed the arrest of a Palestinian suspect. The respondents did not know this at the time of the interview.)

The majority of respondents had not seen the documentary. As with the two clips above, most respondents were upset by the clip, but – in this case – the strength of their upset was marked. Over half the sample said that they were 'very upset' by the clip and a further quarter said that they were 'slightly upset'.

**Table 20. Reactions to the documentary clip**

|  | % |
| --- | --- |
| Very upset | 57 |
| Slightly upset | 26 |
| Not at all | 14 |
| Don't know | 4 |

Nearly a third of the respondents said that they had been particularly upset by the unnecessary violence or the brutality of the scene and 17 per cent said they were upset by the forcible arrest of the man. Again, women mentioned the detail of the clip more often than did men.

*Comparison of clips*

Respondents were asked to consider which clip was the most upsetting. Over one-half of the respondents said that they found the third clip, taken from the documentary, the most upsetting. Ray Fitzwalter, later in the Review, talks of the importance of showing the viewer 'the proper purpose of violence' in a documentary. If this is done, he says, it will be accepted. It is clear that the violence in the documentary clip that was shown to these respondents – which included the cameraman's justification (or purpose) in filming it – was too great for this audience and could not be exonerated.

Nearly one-third said that they found the reconstruction the most likely to upset while the remainder (13 per cent) mentioned the news bulletin.

The sample was then asked to consider each clip again, and to state whether it would be more or less acceptable if it had belonged to another genre. The results are presented in Table 21.

### Table 21. Genre and acceptability

|  | More % | Less % | No difference % |
|---|---|---|---|
| *Reconstruction* | | | |
| As news | 22 | 16 | 62 |
| As documentary | 16 | 10 | 73 |
| *News* | | | |
| As reconstruction | 13 | 26 | 60 |
| As documentary | 16 | 11 | 73 |
| *Documentary* | | | |
| As reconstruction | 18 | 22 | 60 |
| As news | 21 | 15 | 64 |

When considering factual programmes, it can be seen that the genre of the programme clip seen did not in fact alter respondents' views significantly about the acceptability of that clip. The news was the only programme type that began to close the acceptability gap because respondents appeared to afford it greater licence. Even so, it was the content of the clip that ultimately governed how acceptable it was.

## Conclusions

The prime conclusion of any survey of this kind, which considers issues affecting the audience, is that viewers are concerned about the level of violence on television. They not only feel that there is too much violence but they are also unsure how the images seen might impact on the viewer.

Certainly this consideration of factual violence showed that respondents could be very upset by the images presented. Although it might be said that 'violence is violence', regardless of the genre in which it fell, factual programmes raised questions about the respondents' own physical limitations, about the society in which they lived, and about concern for others. Fiction allowed a suspension of belief, however closely one became involved in the storyline – that luxury was not afforded to the viewer of non-fiction. Further, violence in fiction was often felt to be unnecessary and exaggerated and so divorced from reality. (It must be said, however, that the fictional violence which most upset tended to be violence placed in a context most like the viewer's own world.)

Violence in factual television was more acceptable because it was real, and here the dilemma respondents faced is once again clear. They felt actual violence was a fact of life and so should be shown for reasons of duty or information – but the fact that it did reflect the 'real world' made it more upsetting than fictional violence.

The inclusion of dramatic techniques in factual programmes such as reconstructions or documentaries, could heighten the upset caused to the viewer by confusing the parameters set for factual programmes. These parameters insisted that purpose was shown – that the violent images were an illustration of an item reported – and that certain criteria, such as certainty of the outcome, the showing of the minimum number of images, and so on were all adhered to. Should dramatic techniques be included which blurred these parameters then the distress caused to the respondent could be increased.

Respondents were prepared to offer the news most licence in the level of violent images it could show. However, many respondents did not seem to be aware of a Watershed for the news and called for greater restraint in the images shown. This is not to say that they asked for the news to be sanitized. Respondents accepted the importance of the news and insisted that the truth be told and shown. Indeed, most of the respondents were avid viewers of the news. However, the content determined how much of the image should be shown (cf. reactions to the documentary clip) and even the news had to work within the broad boundaries set for all factual programmes.

The respondents underlined, as they have done in all the Council's surveys, the need to warn viewers about material to be transmitted so that they could prepare themselves. But there were still limitations on the extent to which warnings could relieve the upset caused, for, as we shall see further in the next section on the editing groups, some images or programmes were not considered justifiable, even with warnings and whatever the context.

Finally, the respondents' own sense of vulnerability should be mentioned again for it was this which seemed to define many of the responses found in this quantified stage and was apparent in the editing groups. Female respondents seemed very aware of and concerned with the violence around them, and on television, as were those respondents who were becoming older. This concern had little relationship with exposure to violence – the younger male respondents, most likely to have experienced violence in some way, were less threatened by it when presented with images on their television screens, regardless of whether it was real or fictional violence.

# 2. Detailed Findings of the Editing Groups

by David E. Morrison and Brent MacGregor
with Andrew Thorpe

*Institute of Communications Studies, University of Leeds*

## Introduction

'Crime' and 'Violence' were the answers overwhelmingly given by respondents in discussions in different parts of the country to the question, 'What bothers you most when you look around at society today?'

That research was conducted by the Institute of Communications Studies at Leeds University. In undertaking the present study for the Broadcasting Standards Council, the Institute brought together groups of viewers to take part in editing sessions, but did not immediately reveal to them that the sessions were concerned with the presentation of violence on television. To establish whether they shared the concerns of viewers elsewhere, the respondents were first asked the question already described. The dominant answers were, again, 'Crime' and 'Violence'.

> *Basically all the trouble that's going on – robberies that are going on, the general youth that don't seem to give two monkeys about anybody else or anybody else's property, things like that. I think everybody will be a bit uptight about that. Crime and violence generally.*
> (Man, 40–55 years old)

> *Violence, sloppiness, the youngsters just moping around not doing anything. Vandalising, joyriding, the destructiveness.*
> (Woman, 55+ years old)

What became clear, and of central importance to this research, was the 'idea' that violence is textured; it is not necessary for something to be violent to convey messages of violence. For example, in discussing violence on television, one woman satellite viewer said that it was crime that bothered her the most, and then went on to say that she thought there was too much violence, *'not so much on telly but videos'* and she complained bitterly about the level of swearing: *'it's all swearing, isn't it, in a lot of them?'* When challenged that swearing was not violence, she replied, *'But it leads to it, doesn't it, swearing is getting angry, comes to violence'.*

Very few of the respondents had personally experienced violence, but several had been burgled. In general, they did not associate burglary with violence, probably for the reason that when it occurred they were not at home. Words such as 'intrusion' were used to describe how they felt. One man, however, aged about forty-five, who had been burgled when he was present said that he did associate violence with burglary. And the reason: *'Because I hit him'.*

We will see later that attitudes to violence in everyday life colour attitudes to violence on television. This particular man, for example, had been, by his own confession, a violent person in his younger days, and showed an extreme tolerance to violence on television. While hardly anyone in the groups considered that the untransmitted pictures from the war in Bosnia (examined in this research) should have been shown at all, he thought that they could be shown on a children's programme, *Newsround*.

William Belson (*Television Violence and the Adolescent Boy*, 1978), in his massive correlation study of the effects of violent programming, demonstrates a relationship between the viewing of violent programmes and violent behaviour. Although a range of criticisms has been levelled at this study, one of the most telling against the claim that violent adolescents tend to watch more violent programmes than their non-violent counterparts is the observation that violent people tend to like violent programmes: a disposition to violence prompted the heavy viewing of violent programmes and not the reverse.

The attraction held by violent programmes for violent people may be the case in terms of fictional programmes, but there is good reason to doubt, given the evidence of the editing exercises described here, whether this holds true for factual programmes. Although those who had a 'tough attitude' to social violence, and indeed indicated that they were not unfamiliar with actual violence, were not easily shocked by what they saw, they did not show any particular wish for factual programmes to be enhanced with violence. In fact, those who especially appreciated fictional violence – and these were mainly satellite women viewers – did not wish to extend their enjoyment of violence to the consumption of it in factual programmes. In short, the rules governing the portrayal of violence in non-fiction would appear to differ from those governing violence in fiction. Why this should be so we will see shortly, but basically the judgement of real life violence on television includes a different set of moral judgements than that governing fictional violence.

The indication that swearing might be considered as violence alerted the researchers to the role that language might play in the viewer's response to violence in factual programmes. Indeed, the relationship of words and pictures did turn out to be very important in judging whether or not scenes were acceptable. The violence does not have to be graphic to be found 'disturbing'.

The research used a technique, specifically developed by the Institute, that allowed respondents to edit for themselves scenes of factual violence. The new method allowed researchers not only to observe closely their decision-making process in deciding between acceptable and non-acceptable scenes, but also allowed the respondents to be questioned closely about their reasons for re-editing the material.

The business of editing made quite clear which parts of the material the respondents wanted to include or exclude, but what was harder to determine was how the findings might be interpreted to show their concerns about violence. The researchers had to create a framework which would account for the differences in responses.

In addition to the consideration of the social factors which gave rise to the acceptability of violence, the material generated by the research forced us to confront the very difficult question of what the respondents understood by reality. The research had revealed a weaving between fictional and non-fictional accounts of the world. But did viewers slide about in a state of confusion as to what was real and what was not?

It is a question we would, by intellectual preference, wished to have left alone. Yet close contact with the respondent showed that providing an answer to such a question could not be avoided. We were interested in responses to factual violence, but respondents found it impossible to consider such real violence without reference to fiction.

The report, therefore, covers a wide range of questions, not just about factual violence, but about how the viewer stands in relation to television and the images of the real and the fictional that it carries. One thing is for sure, what we see may not be a new type of viewer, but a new type of understanding of the viewer informed by the way in which they viewed factual violence.

## The sample

All groups were recruited by the professional recruitment agency QRS. Ten groups were recruited from the socio-economic groups C1/C2, split for age and sex. These groups each consisted of 7–8 respondents and were conducted between 18 March and 1 April 1993:

- 16-24 year old men
- 16-24 year old women
- 25-34 year old men
- 25-34 year old women
- 40-55 year old men
- 40-55 year old women
- 55+ year old men
- 55+ year old women
- under 50 satellite viewers, men
- under 50 satellite viewers, women

## The material edited

The material used was chosen to include as wide a range as possible of factual violence from a variety of broadcasting organizations whose output was widely available in the United Kingdom. Research identified several discrete areas for exploration.

## *Types of violence*

### *1. Actual violence*

*Cops*, shown on Sky 1, the British Sky Broadcasting channel. Shot in fly-on-the-wall style, real violence captured by a film crew working with American police.

### *2. Victims of violence*

A local news item about a man whose ear was bitten off in a street brawl. This was an instance both of the physical results of violence being shown, and of the journalistic description of an actual violent event which made it an instance also of *reported violence*.

### *3. Perpetrators of violence*

An extract from the Central Television documentary, *Viewpoint 93*, 'Murder in Mind' (which was about serial killers) transmitted on the ITV Network, 27 January 1993 at 10.40 pm. The clip consisted mainly of an interview with Dennis Nilsen about his crimes.

### *4. Reconstructions of violence*

- *Crimewatch UK* (BBC 1 December 10 1992, 9.30 pm) a dramatic reconstruction of a violent attack on a woman which included an actual contemporary photograph of her wounds and an interview with the victim inter-cut with the reconstruction. The piece therefore included a *victim of violence*.

- *World in Action*, 'Dennis the Menace', transmitted on the ITV Network (27 July 1992, 8.30 pm). In this extract a reconstruction of torture was inter-cut with the testament of the victim's friend.

### *5. Actual violence captured on the screen by news cameras in the course of reporting*

In this context the issue is how much violence is necessary to tell the story in question. Two instances were chosen.

- A documentary, called *The Eye of the Storm* about combat cameramen transmitted on BBC2 November 7 1992 at 8.05 pm. This film showed classic news footage of the Vietnam war. Included were two well-known sequences: a naked girl running away having being burnt by napalm and a Vietcong suspect being summarily executed by the Saigon Chief of Police. Both of these instances are specifically referred to in the BBC's 1987 Guidelines for Producers:

Do not allow such images to become a reach-me-down shorthand for great conflicts, e.g. the South Vietnamese General shooting a prisoner or the napalmed children fleeing their village to signify the Vietnam War.
(*Violence on Television: Guidelines for Production Staff*, BBC, 1987, p.10)

- A *BBC News* report transmitted on 17 February 1993 from former Yugoslavia about alleged atrocities in Bosnia that had been discovered by Serbian forces. It was *reported violence*, showing the consequences of violence rather than actual violent events. In addition to the material transmitted on BBC1, respondents were shown untransmitted material of the same event which the broadcaster had excluded on grounds of taste and decency.

These seven extracts offered a wide range of possible audience response on a number of related issues. There was a clear opportunity for minute, detailed re-editing down to the level of individual shots and words. In addition other current material was available to be shown to any group who might have mentioned these incidents. This material was not shown to every group as a matter of course.

Every effort was made to give all of the pieces shown to the groups their proper context. Respondents were told which programme the sequences were from and the time of the day they would have been transmitted. The aim was to set the extract that respondents were being shown in the context of the wider purpose of the programme from which it came.

## Viewer editing results

### Cops

#### (i) Description of extract

The first material shown to groups was an extract from the American programme, *Cops*. This material was shot in the *cinema verité*, 'fly-on-the-wall' style typical of the series, transmitted on Saturday evenings starting at 9.00 pm. At the beginning of each programme of *Cops* there is an on-screen caption: 'Due to the graphic nature of this programme, viewer discretion is advised'. This warning is not read out.

In the chosen sequence, a man is being chased by the police. The whole incident takes place at night, making exact details very hard to make out. The camera work is shaky. There is no dialogue or voice-over and the actuality sound is both loud and imprecise. The entire sequence is virtually one long hand-held shot. The suspect is cornered against a fence where he is attacked by a police dog. He wrestles with the dog and with some of the police officers who at one point are seen to hit him. He is eventually subdued, but the whole incident is chaotic and perceptibly quite violent. The suspect's trousers are torn and the police dog is clearly seen biting him. There is a shot near the end of the sequence which shows details of a wound to what seems to be the suspect's arm.

*(ii) Initial response and editing*

One member of the 16–24 year old male group saw some public service point in *Cops*, saying that it gave some idea of the pressures the police worked under. Most of the group, however, felt that it was *'kind of sick'* that such material was intended as entertainment television, particularly scheduled, as it was, on Saturday nights in prime time.

One group member actually said, *'Oh, I bet you I know what the titles look like'*, and he proceeded to describe very accurately the title sequence of the programme, right down to the style of music chosen.

The 25–34 year old men, whose own personal experience of violence was high, thought that *Cops* was sensationalized, and they saw no point in showing it. They thought that the fly-on-the-wall style of filming was acceptable, but as a piece of television programme-making they did not particularly think that the banal every-day violence of the *Cops* sequence was one they would want to see. They said it certainly should not be in a weekly programme, although it was perhaps acceptable as part of a one-off documentary. They demanded context, wanting to know what the fugitive had done. Interestingly the 25–34 year old female group, although they found it personally upsetting, were happier to see the material transmitted, provided it was post-Watershed.

Many of these comments were echoed by the 40–55 year old male group, one of whom added programmes like that should not be made on the grounds that television can create the event, that the policemen being filmed could act up so that the event was unconsciously dramatized for the camera. The group said they could spot the difference between factual programming and fiction, usually from technical clues.

The only substantive editing change made to this material was to remove the detailed close-up of the arm wound.

Two different reasons were given for this request. Some members of the 40–55 year old and 55+ year old male groups and some satellite viewing males removed the close-up of the wound because it was disturbing. The 55+ year old men said that this cut *'softened it,'* but it still did not make the material suitable for pre-Watershed transmission. The 25–34 year old male group edited the wound out, not for reasons of taste, but because it was clearly an intervention by the cameraman and editor. This well-informed comment on television techniques was not typical however.

Many respondents simply did not want to see the programme. Two main reasons were given. Some in the groups objected personally to the violence, while others did not see the point of such material. Many were careful to point out, however, that such a decision was personal and not tantamount to saying it should not be shown. The violence-tolerant satellite viewing female group who thought the programme was transmitted to increase ratings, nevertheless felt that it did help 'kids' to learn about the real world.

*(iii) Further responses*

*(a) Men 16–24 years old:* This clip was certainly seen as violent by the respondents but, as one of the 16-24 year old men commented:

> Can you really call it violence though? O.K. there was one shot where you could actually hear the butt of the gun going against the guy's head, but I'm not very sure whether you could call it violence. I mean what is violence? It wasn't TV violence, it was real violence.

The query about whether the violence in *Cops* ought to be considered violence is interesting, and so is the comment, *'it gets you quite excited'*. Violence of the type shown by *Cops* was clearly associated with drama. The excitement of such violence stemmed from the fact that the outcome of proceedings was unknown – *'it just kept going and going'*. Indeed, the viewer is carried along with the event. Yet we already see, from the above quotes, a challenge to the purpose of the programme – 'is it entertainment or is it real life?'

Although no-one in this age group mistook the sequence as a drama or even a dramatic reconstruction, it seemed to them to lack any integrity of purpose that could exclude it from being entertainment. The fact that it was given a prime-time Saturday evening slot convinced them that the point of the violence was to attract an audience through its entertainment value.

None of the groups had any particular objection to the level of violence portrayed in *Cops*, nor did many people confuse the programme with other genres, apart, that is, from the women aged 40-55.

*(b) Women 40–55 years old:* Even though we had mentioned that *Cops* was a fly-on-the-wall programme, these women were unsure about its status. Asked immediately after the showing, 'what they thought of that', one woman queried, *'was that for real, was it news or something?'* When told that it was a filmed real event, she replied, *'I wanted to make sure ... these things, you never know if it is for real or not'*. Asked, 'if it wasn't for real what might it have been?', she replied, *'I thought it was probably a film or a documentary'*.

The lighting was so poor in the clip that we were puzzled that this fact alone might not have suggested it was not a film. This woman replied, *'No, not at night, I wouldn't have thought so'*.

The reason for the confusion as to whether *Cops* was a film or not appeared to stem from the fact of the disorganized arrest and the number of officers that it took to restrain one man: actuality did not conform to their ideas of reality. However, none of the women thought that the scene required editing; although one woman did say, *'If anything had happened to the dog, I would have wanted that cutting out'*. Asked why, she answered, *'Because it is not the dog's fault. It is trained to do that'*.

Although concern for the dog might be taken as sentimentality towards the canine world, it nevertheless embodies an important point about the portrayal of violence in factual programmes; namely, the guilt or status of the individuals portrayed – in this case a dutiful dog – influences the acceptance of the degree or extent of violence that is shown.

When asked to consider the sequence in which the suspect's wounds are shown, (the shot some groups edited out), these women decided that they did not wish to edit it out.

The judgement of the acceptability of violence in factual programmes entails a high degree of moral involvement. For violence to be acceptable, it must be seen to have a point and purpose to be included in the programme, but respondents also apply a concept of justice to the acts that take place. At no point in the extract had we been informed what the arrested man was supposed to have done. Had he been a rapist, for example, then the horror of his crime would have downgraded the horror of any injury that he may have suffered in the course of his apprehension, and made the viewing of any injury, such as a wound to the throat, acceptable to these respondents. The psychological underpinnings of this acceptance of the portrayal of graphic injury may be simple: the lack of sympathy with the victim (the suspect in this case) means a lack of emotional caring, which then reduces the impact of the violence. The moral tale of 'goodies' and 'baddies' exists in factual as well as fiction programmes. These women in particular showed themselves to be deeply moved by instances of human suffering. The depth of their caring was matched, however, by not caring what happened to the perpetrators of the suffering, especially if the suffering involved children. This attitude was reflected again in the willingness of the male over fifty-five group to change their views about the acceptability of violence according to what they considered the person arrested to have done.

*(c) Men 55+ years old:* It was agreed by the group that the film was violent: '*It was quite frightening, extremely violent*'. When pressed about what made it violent, the response from one man was, '*I think mainly the police attitude, I know whatever he has done he doesn't want treating like that*'.

He thought, as most of this group did, that the picture of the wounded arm (it is unclear whether it is a leg or an arm) ought to be edited from the film. The violence was unnecessary because, in his opinion, there were sufficient police to restrain the man without the assistance of a dog. However, he went on to say:

> *If he was resisting arrest, which he obviously was, he deserves everything he gets. If someone came into your home and violated it you wouldn't care a damn if the police beat him up.*

Even though attitudes shifted in light of what crime was supposed to have been committed, most still considered the level of violence shown unacceptable. The film was duly edited. On re-showing the edited version, the response was:

> *It softens it a bit. We know that he has been arrested, presumably his hands are behind his back, and we haven't seen the leg. I don't think there is any need for it in actual fact. It is much more acceptable like that.*

> *Although the edited version was more acceptable, the programme itself was not really approved of. This group failed to see the purpose of such a programme: 'I've no idea [of the purpose] to be honest. I don't see the point'. A pointless programme meant that the violence shown was pointless.*

*(d) Female satellite viewers:* The group which particularly enjoyed *Cops* were the women viewers of satellite television. Many were fans of *Cops* and watched it

regularly. It was viewed and enjoyed as entertainment while, as we have seen, the general view in the other groups was that the programme lacked a valid purpose and thus the violence in it, although not considered especially shocking, could not be justified. As one of the women aged 16–24 had said in discussing what shots to take out:

> I'd take out all of them. Not that it's shocking or I disapprove, but I'm really not that interested. I'd just rather not see it. If it had been broadcast on the news, as news, then it would be different but I don't need to see it to know it goes on. And we don't know what he's done so we can't judge.

In other words, for it to be acceptable as a news item the story would have had to have a context to conform to accepted news values.

*(e) Men 24–35 years old:* The men aged 24–35 also considered that the violence in *Cops* had little point. They did, however, consider that the violence would have been acceptable in a documentary, but only because it would be a 'one-off' and not part of a series of such programmes:

> If it is a one-off documentary keep it in, if it's not it's just sensationalizing.

What we witness is the idea that the scene shown in *Cops* would be valid if it was a news item – that the violence would be part of a larger story – and that it would also have been valid in a documentary if it was a 'one-off' programme about police work. As a regular series on the police the violence shown lost its claim for inclusion on the grounds that it was felt to be included simply to attract audiences for further shows. It was drama by another name.

## Local News

### (i) Description of extract

The next piece shown to groups was a local news item about a court case transmitted in 1992 by Television South. This extract was chosen because it was an instance of reporting violence, including the graphic display of its consequences, rather than actual on-screen violence. Respondents were shown a report of a court case in which the verdict had just been handed down. In addition to the straightforward reporter's piece to camera outside the courtroom so often seen, this item consisted of a still photograph of the man who had been sentenced, some general shots of the scene of the crime and various shots of the victim who had had his ear bitten off. These ranged from some general views of him walking down the street to detailed close-ups of the side of his head showing the healed wound where his ear had been. There was no interview with the victim, although he appeared in an interview-like situation, shot over the shoulder of the reporter, but he was never heard actually speaking. The transcript of the item ran as follows:

| | |
|---|---|
| 1. B/w still* of accused (Winton) | VO ... the court being told of a gruesome fight which the judge described as quite appalling violence. Winton's victim was Channel Tunnel electrician, Pat Neary, |

2. CU stub of ear, now healed. Zoom out to head and shoulders of victim

who lost an ear and nearly his sight in the fight in October last year.

3. Ext. winebar sign, zoom out to WS ext. winebar

Winton had confronted Neary in Bluffs Wine Bar in Dover. Winton had stripped to the waist to fight,

4. Ext. street in front of winebar

the pair falling down steps to the street. There Winton tried to gouge out Mr. Neary's eyes.

5. Reporter piece to camera

Mr. Neary told the court – 'the pain you cannot imagine. I thought I was going to lose my right eye. I tried to get away out of sheer panic and self-preservation'. But Winton hadn't finished.

6. Still as 1 above

He then delivered a chilling message and calmly said, 'I'm going to bite your ear off'. He sank his teeth into

7. Over the shoulder shot of victim talking to reporter

Mr. Neary's right ear and tore it off. In court Mr. Neary described a ripping sensation but he was blind as to what was happening to him.

8. Reporter PTC as 5

When Mr. Neary's eyes had recovered he saw his attacker standing over him. He spat the ear onto the floor and said, 'there's your ear back'.

9. WS victim walking down street toward camera

Mr. Neary's ear was packed in ice after the fight and he was taken to hospital. Doctors have implanted it in his leg.

10. CU stub of ear as 1

There are hopes it'll grow more blood vessels to be grafted onto the side of his head later.

11. Colour still of judge

The judge, Mr. Justice Rook, said Winton was guilty of hideous injuries, causing a scar the victim will carry for the rest of his life.

12. Reporter PTC as 5, 8

The court was told that Winton was a former boxer, soldier and night club bouncer. As the sentence was handed out more than a dozen of his friends left the court in silence.

*For a description of the technical terms used, refer to Appendix 2.

*(ii) Initial response and editing*

Many groups found this report sensationalized the events. It was frequently re-edited with two particular aspects receiving attention. Individual phrases used by the reporter were removed, as was the repeated use of close-ups showing the now healed wound.

The 16–24 year old males took out two close-ups of the healed wound and removed some of the descriptions they considered sensational. They did however use the detailed close-up of the damaged ear at the end of the report where they thought it was used in a better context. Interestingly, they took out other shots that they thought were extraneous, including daylight views of the exterior of the night club (3, 4). An over-the-shoulder shot of the reporter speaking to the victim (7) was removed as its sound track consisted of reporter voice-over rather than the expected words of the interviewee. They also edited out two separate phrases that the reporter had used. They would have liked to have heard more testimony from the actual victim himself who did appear, but never spoke. They appeared to want the report neutralized.

Other groups concurred generally, removing the repeated use of the close-up of the ear. The 16–24 year old females simplified the piece, toning down the script and using only the still of the convicted man (1), the reporter's piece to camera (5) and the over-the-shoulder shot of the victim talking to the reporter (7), which showed the ear but in significantly less detail than the close-ups.

Similarly, the 55+ year old males removed the close-up of the ear (2), took out the exterior shots of the winebar (3,4) as well as a still of the judge (11). The 55+ year old females removed the close-up of the ear, the wine bar shot and, additionally, the shot of the victim walking down the street (9). They had found the piece as broadcast to be sensational, disgusting and horrifying and wished 'to clean up' the script. Only the 25–34 year old men who had all 'seen worse' found the transmitted version totally acceptable.

- Phrases edited out of TVS script:

16–24 year old male      'to gouge out Mr. Neary's eyes'
                                         'delivered a chilling message'

40–55 year old female      'to gouge out Mr. Neary's eyes'
                                         'sheer panic'
                                         'He sank his teeth into Mr. Neary's right ear and tore it off'
                                         'Mr. Neary described a ripping sensation'
                                         'He spat the ear onto the floor'

55+ year old female      'gouge out Mr. Neary's eyes'
                                         'He sank his teeth into Mr. Neary's right ear and tore it off'

55+ year old male      'He spat the ear onto the floor and said here is your ear back'
                                         'Mr. Neary described a ripping sensation'
                                         'The court was told that Winton was a former boxer, soldier and night club bouncer.'

*(iii) Further responses*

*(a) Men 24–35 years old:* Although the men aged 24–35 were not shocked by the scene in *Cops* – they did not consider it especially violent – it became clear, when showing them the TVS news report, why pictures of real life violence did not affect them much. In the opening discussion they accepted the news as necessarily entailing scenes of violence: *'I think they are just portraying what is happening in the world. If that's the state of the world, then that's what we expect in a democracy, to see it'*. But it was also clear that some of the men in the group, because of their familiarity with violence in everyday life, were unmoved by 'domestic' violent images in the news that others found shocking.

Indeed, they considered the victim was probably partly responsible for his own misfortune.

> *This guy [victim] works in the Channel Tunnel, he earns a few bob. Big lad.*

> *You didn't know what the motivation was for the fight in the first place. This fellow might have been, you know, ten times more superior mentally than the fellow who ripped his ear off – he might have been much more guilty of committing mental violence to that chap, goading him. You know, the guy who actually done it to him ... retribution.*

There is a Hobbesian sense of justice here in that the intellectually inferior man was perhaps right to use naked physical aggression to get the better of the other man. Certainly, the physical appearance of the victim, his size and the fact that he worked in a well-paid job cutting the Channel Tunnel, all made for evidence in judging not just the rightness of the attack but the horror of the injury. He was not seen as an innocent.

This group did not wish to edit anything out of the sequence:

> *We are supposed to be talking about how it was reported and I think that was about right. That is on the 6 pm news and midday news and is acceptable. I think that showing the injury and reading out the description of the attack, it was relevant. It wasn't just stuck in there for sensation.*

A central principle can be drawn from the above comment and one which is found to be universally applicable – the closer to real life factual programmes are, the less they should sensationalize the events or happenings covered. News, in so far as these respondents were concerned, was the purest form of factual programming, and hence the area that, above all, ought not to sensationalize.

Even so, this group of men were unusual in not wishing to make any edits to this particular item. The explanation rests in the fact that they were familiar with this kind of violent situation. To them, the description of the fight given by the reporter and the injury shown was an accurate description of 'reality'. Furthermore, and this supports the point made earlier about sympathy with a victim influencing the impact of imagery, these men felt little sympathy with the victim.

*(b) Men 16–24 years old:* The youngest men, aged 16–24, were entirely different from the 24–35 year old men in their response. They appeared not to be so familiar in their

everyday life with violence as the older men were. After viewing the item, one of the men said:

> *Shocking. It's very graphic the way it's described – 'gouged' and 'tore off' and so on, it's very complete language. It's a combination of both – the pictures and the way it is worded and the timing – that makes it shocking.*

This man's reaction to the news story is a classic example of the limitations of content analysis in capturing the content of any audio/visual text. Why this item shocked him was not just the visual images, nor the actual verbal description but the inflection in the reporter's voice in describing the events. The script was given to each viewer to read and comment upon. After reading it they agreed that the account when given in cold print did not have the same power to shock: *'When you read that written down it is not quite as bad as he delivered it. It was delivered to sound really dramatic'.*

No-one in the group thought the story would be complete without the picture of the missing ear, and thus debate took place concerning how best to feature it.

> *Do you need it in the first shot, or is it best at the end where they are going on about it being grafted back on, that would be better actually, it would make more sense.*

The main point to note in their comments was the phrase, *'it would make more sense'*, when referring to where the picture of the ear ought to come in the report. These respondents wanted sense and context, not sensation.

It is worth noting that one of the men particularly liked the ending of this news item in that, for him, it carried a moral lesson: *'I liked the bit at the end when he said his [the attacker's] friends left the court in silence, that was good, as though in disgrace'.* However, someone else criticized the story in that it did not give sufficient attention to the sentence:

> *I think they're more interested in what the story was about rather than the sentence. The report doesn't show that justice is being done.*

His comment is a call for the news when covering such incidents to regard it fully as a crime story which ought to have as its thrust and conclusion the apprehension and punishment of the offender and not the sensationalizing/glorification of the crime itself.

*(c) Men 40–45 years old:* These men had little objection to the item, although the group was somewhat split in its 'sensitivity to violence'. It was quite clear that some members were shocked by the statements made by others in the group, and some had been disturbed by the *Cops* film: *'It frightens me because it is real, it's not like a fictional programme that you can think, well at the end of the day they are only actors, that is real. It does feel worse, it gives me the jitters'.*

There was no doubt, however, that the overwhelming consensus was that the report was sensational, yet what restricted the horror of this particular news item for these respondents was their estimation of the character of the two participants to the fracas. Indeed, like the men aged 24–35, one felt that these men could easily place the type of characters involved in the fight within their own sphere of direct personal knowledge. They were keen to judge the participants in the fight and felt that the report had cast the victim too much in the role of the innocent party, especially by the use of a black-and-white picture for the convicted party and colour pictures for the victim.

The shock value of the violence was diminished because it was felt that such behaviour could be expected from the characters involved. When asked, would the pictures have been more shocking if the injured person had been someone like a school teacher, the response was, 'Well, it would have been, wouldn't it?' The suggestion that a school teacher would frequent such a place as that where the fight took place struck a chord of incredulity: 'In fact, I don't think the situation would have arisen, because a school teacher wouldn't be in such a fight like that'.

(d) Men 55+ years old: The fifty-five plus men had little of the cavalier attitude to violence that some of the younger men exhibited. The infirmity of some of the men made them wary of what they saw as a brutish world.

Their response to the news report was most certain. 'Horrendous', was the response of one man. Asked what made it horrendous, he replied:

> Firstly, to almost blind a man in a fight and then admit he was going to bite his ear off, I think that is absolutely horrendous. It just shocks so many people. It's something akin to the previous thing [Cops] so far as the injury to the ear can be compared to the injury to the leg.

There was no suggestion among these older men that the story should not have been covered. Their objection was to the level of injury shown and the manner of its reportage. Again, we see that language describing violence can be as disturbing as actual pictures of violence.

> I would have said severe injuries to the head, without going into all the detail. You can just say someone got his ear bitten off, you don't want pictures of it.

This group discussed in great detail what shots should be included in the story:

> You have got two shots of the eye and the ear ... you have one shot of the ear, that's bad enough without having to see a close-up of it. That doesn't look as bad. Leave that in but take the close-up out – that one is horrendous, that poor guy looks horrendous enough there.

What is interesting here is that the victim is referred to as 'that poor guy'. Such sentiments were entirely missing from the previous groups. The reactions of this older group of men lends support to the thesis that the registering of horror and demand for exclusion is determined to a certain extent by levels of sympathy towards the victim or injured party.

(e) Women 16–24 years old: The young women, aged 16–24, introduced a new element into the discussion of the report, but one that was to surface later in discussing the Viewpoint film, namely the value of information in relation to the position of the viewer. The women of this group considered that the detail which was given, and the explicitness of the scenes shown, might be valuable and relevant to a jury, but not to the ordinary viewer. They wished, therefore, for severe editing.

> As viewers we don't need to know all that, we're not the jury, they need that information. There is really no need for us to know it.

(f) *Women 25–34 years old:* The 25–34 year old women were like their male counter-parts in their viewing of violence. They also showed themselves to savour violent retribution in cases such as rape or child molesting. One woman, wishing to separate herself from the enthusiasm for rough justice, dissented and, with what was an apparent strong commitment to due process of law, said:

> *If it was my child that had been molested I would react violently, but the police are supposed to be law-abiding people, so they shouldn't commit violence if it is not necessary.*

This group were specifically asked if the pictures *'made them squirm'*. They replied that they did not, but they did criticize the presentation for being too detailed and showing too many pictures of the close-up of the healed wound. Their objection to the film, however, appeared to be on grounds of professional competence: you saw the ear too many times, *'poor man he has lost his ear and doesn't want all the world to see it'*.

The reference to *'poor man'* here is not resonant with the same type of sympathy expressed by the term *'poor guy'* used by the over fifty-five year old men of the previous group. It is more a reference to some kind of cosmetic misfortune that one would not wish the rest of the world to see in close-up, or repeatedly, rather than sympathy for any pain he may have suffered in the course of losing his ear.

(g) *Women 55+ years old:* The over fifty-five year old women were the most sensitive of all groups to the portrayal of violence. Like the 55+ year old men, age, and the decreasing confidence in one's ability to respond to physical danger, appeared to have produced a nervousness in these women. They felt vulnerable to attack or harassment.

> *I have never actually seen any violence, but you're wary. I sort of feel there's someone behind me even when I walk my dog, but I still keep walking my dog without any problems.*

While age may have reduced their feeling that they might be able to protect them-selves from attack, they also blamed their nervousness on the age that we live in:

> *I think it's the age where you get more aware of the violence that's about. Whereas at one time our age group could walk about and no-one would bother you. It's the young ones that are growing up, and the girls are as bad as the boys. A lot of muggings are intended on older people.*

The group thought there were too many shots of the damaged head, and particularly wanted some of 'the close-up' of the missing ear taken out. *'You can see what the reporter is talking about ... it [the damaged head] should be shown to let you know what the reporter is actually talking about'*. Thus, they were not in favour of having no shots of the head, but they were most insistent in altering the description of the fight:

> *We think it could be worded better, it's crude, sickening, like an animal. Does it have to be described 'he sank his teeth in and tore it off' we've already heard what has happened.*

They wished to remove *'gouged his eyes'* substituting *'attacked his eyes, went for his eyes'*. *'And we'd remove the bit where it says 'he spat out the ear on the floor'*. The alterations duly made to their video prompted the consideration that it was fit for *Calendar*, Yorkshire Television's local news programme. They understood that the report was a news item and that the real world had to be reported: *'Yes, it's a news item, but the description didn't make it any better news'*.

*(h) Female satellite viewers:* These respondents appeared not to be shocked by violence at all; (perhaps) partly accounted for by the entertainment value they extracted from it. They discussed the TVS news report in an entirely different manner from any of the other groups.

> *I think the presentation of it was disgraceful before you start, because he [reporter] didn't do it right. I don't think the scene with the ear sort of made any difference, you weren't shocked by the shot without the ear.*

While other groups had criticized the way the reporter handled the story, this group appeared to criticize him for spoiling the story.

> *They need another reporter. It sounds like a put-up does that. His ear got bit off and blah blah. It's just the way he said it as well. It's more like a police report rather than part of the telly.*

They did think the still of the judge ought to be edited out on the grounds that, *'it doesn't matter what the judge said, you know a judge is a judge, you don't have to see his face'*.

The attitude of these women to violence clearly does make them somewhat different from members of the other groups. Although there may be a few explanations for this – and we will see later that they have what must be, at least statistically, a particular fascination with violence – the reason that they subscribed to satellite television was entertainment.

*(i) Male satellite viewers:* The male satellite viewers, who mainly watched the sport on satellite, were markedly different from their female counterparts in their acceptance of violence. They had not considered *Cops* especially appealing, nor did they find it exciting. Their reactions to this item were similar to those expressed by many of the terrestrial viewers.

> *Terrible. I think that should have been on a bit later myself. I think there was a bit too much for early TV. The ear was shown at least three times there.*

It would seem that not only was the item, as transmitted, considered unsuitable for early evening viewing, but that the graphic detail was *'unnecessary for an adult news'*. They definitely wished the programme to be edited.

The debate over where best to include the injury revolved around reducing the dramatic impact of the wound. Although two respondents disagreed with this, a cogent argument was put by one man for including the controversial picture at the beginning of the item: *'I think showing it without going into graphic detail before showing it, and you just show somebody with his ear missing, makes it less dramatic'*.

The detail of the attack was objected to. After reading the script, one man said:

> *It doesn't seem too bad when you're reading it, it's when you're listening to it. I*

*suppose it's his [reporter's] tone as well as style. I think 'he sank his teeth into his right ear and tore it off' ought to have the words changed.*

## Viewpoint '93

*(i) Description of extract*

This extract was from the Central Television documentary 'Murder in Mind' on the subject of serial killers, broadcast at 10.45 pm. The programme included an interview with Dennis Nilsen and had been the subject of legal action until hours before transmission. The programme was preceded by a voice-over warning: 'This film includes an interview with the serial killer Dennis Nilsen which may be disturbing to some viewers'. A second warning which read 'This programme contains pictures and language that many viewers may find disturbing' was written on the screen at the end of the title sequence, some minutes into the programme, following a brief first appearance by Nilsen. A commercial break in the programme was preceded by a short sound bite of the Nilsen interview. During this in-programme trail, two captions, 'Coming Next' and 'Serial Killer Dennis Nilsen's Own Story' appeared consecutively across the bottom of the screen.

Visually speaking, the sequence used was straightforward. General views preceded the interview, including a black and white still of Nilsen at the time of his arrest, with the extract itself consisting of quite a wide shot of him being interviewed in prison. During the interview, there were cutaways to news footage shot at the time of Nilsen's arrest. The two shots in question had been filmed outside the scene of the crimes. One showed a police officer in overalls washing an indeterminate object which could have been a piece of bone, but could equally have been a stone. The second shot was of a plain clothes policeman coming out of the house carrying a large paper sack, the contents of which were unspecified. The transcript ran as follows:

| | |
|---|---|
| 1. B/w still of Nilsen on arrest, zooms into CU profile | V.O: In 1992 Nilsen agreed to be interviewed by Central Television for this programme. The historic film that follows will be used in helping British investigators understand |
| 2. Police van driving away from station with car proceeding, film crews and photographers pursue | the mind of the serial murderer. Nilsen started by disputing how many people he'd killed. |

3. Wide shot on Nilsen speaking to out of vision interviewer

Heading for the police station at the moment of my arrest, they asked me how many there were and I didn't really know, I just gave a figure, and because I was co-operating with the police I decided I would stick with it. So 3 of those victims are invented just to complement the continuity of evidence to the police because then, to keep them happy.

4. CU of bucket, hand enters and removes object, examines it, washes it.

V.O: The dismembered remains of only half a dozen men were found. Nilsen had kept the bodies in cupboards

5. Detective emerges from house carrying paper sack, walks to car and puts sack in boot

or beneath floorboards before disposing of them. Nilsen: In the end there was, when I was, had 2 or 3 bodies under the floorboards, they began to accumulate

6. Nilsen synch int. as 3

so come summer it got hot and I knew there'd be a smell problem. so I had to deal with the smell problem and I thought what would cause the smell more than anything else, and I came to the conclusion it was the innards, the sub-parts of the body, organs and stuff like that. So on a weekend I would so pull up the floorboards, and I found this totally unpleasant and get blinding drunk so I can face it and start the dissection on the kitchen floor. I'd go out and be sick outside in the garden, I mean ...

Out of vision interviewer: What sort of preparation would you have to make for that?
Nilsen: What do you mean preparation?
Int: Well if you were simply to bring these young men's bodies into your kitchen and start to dismember them that's going to leave an awful mess.
Nilsen: No, it doesn't. It doesn't leave a mess. You see when people, in death situations where a knife's involved there's a lot of blood flying around. If I were to

> stab you right now, you could stab
> me, the heart's pumping away
> there, there'd be blood splashing
> all over the place. Funny enough,
> in a dead body there's no blood
> spurts or anything like that, it
> congeals inside and forms part of
> the flesh in man and becomes like
> anything in a butcher's shop,
> there's little or no blood, so
> there's no problem with plastic,
> you know these plastic bags that
> you have.

*(ii) Initial response and editing*

There was a near-unanimous viewer response to this material. Few of the groups wished to edit it, but many did not wish to see it at all. Some, who had seen it on transmission, said it had disturbed them and that the memory had stayed with them far longer than any fictional violence they had seen. Following the rationale offered in the voice-over, several groups independently suggested it should be shown to criminologists and no one else. ' ... *the public wasn't served ... show it to pathologists'* (male satellite viewer). The female satellite viewers, including avid readers of *True Life Crimes* and other similar magazines, actually wanted to edit out the shots of the indeterminate object being washed in the bucket and of the detective carrying out the large paper bag.

*(iii) Further responses*

*(a) Female satellite viewers:* Some of the female satellite viewers had seen the programme at the time of the original transmission. We will come shortly to their comments on the programme, but first it is necessary to establish their interest in the 'macabre'.

> *I get* True Life Crimes, *and he [Nilsen] was in that, actually saying what he was doing with the bodies, and that he sat a body at the side of him on a night-time, and dressed the body. The full case was in and every week there is a different murder. I'll tell you the worst ...*

She was asked the straightforward question, 'Why do you get *True Life Crimes*?':

> *Because we're blood-thirsty really. It has to be said that we want to listen to all these details and we were absolutely shocked – they're one pound twenty five each and it's worth every penny.*

It may well be that listening to bizarre or especially grisly forms of death has a fascination for most people but that is not the same as developing a taste for such material. Two or three of these women showed what can only be described as relish for the obscene aspects of human conduct. And the fact that it was real was its appeal.

The extract that featured Nilsen consisted mainly of him talking about his exploits, of how he cut up his victims and his feelings at the time. This was added to by some news footage of the police taking what were presumably the remains of his victims, or bits of other evidence, away from his house in North London.

> *Do you know what I think was alarming, sick, was you know when they showed you the bits of the body in the water. I think that is absolutely awful. It shouldn't have been shown. Why do they put that on when they know that the victims' relatives are watching?*

The reference to *'the body in the water'* is to a scene where an investigator at Nilsen's house is washing debris – it could be a stone or bone – in a bucket to clear it of dirt. Although this scene caused confusion to quite a few respondents as to the exact nature of what was being washed, this was the most unequivocal statement that it was *'bits of the body'*.

It is noteworthy that at the same time as embellishing the shocking content of the programme, they did not think it right that such scenes should be shown because relatives of the dead might be watching. The taste for violence and a concern for other people existed side by side.

Four members of this group wished for the bucket washing scene to be removed by editing, including one of the magazine readers. It was a puzzle to us why she wanted this removed:

> *Because it is actually showing you. I wouldn't be as shocked if it was in a picture I suppose, but wiping this down and sort of ... it's just there. If it's a photograph it's not actually happening, the photograph's not moving and showing you, it's going into the bucket and washing the piece, and you know that maybe some body, and you can actually see him washing it, and it brings it more to life. When it's in a still, it's more comicified.*

This last quote embodies a vital finding. Although some of these women consumed the most horrid displays of violence and considered *'it was brilliant'*, and also liked graphic fictional violence on television, when it came to factual violence they were not so keen to accept it, even though there was evidence that they found the programme fascinating. It would seem, therefore, that moving images of real life violence are not so readily consumed because they have a reality to them absent in still pictures. However, it must be added that a heavy diet of magazines about real life crime violence might well have assisted these women in bringing the television violence to life through the projection of certainty onto what they were seeing.

*(b) Male satellite viewers:* The male satellite viewers reacted to the film very differently from their female counterparts. Three members of the group thought that the programme ought not to have been shown at all, with a further two who were unsure about their position. This did not demonstrate a willingness to proscribe unpalatable programmes, but rather the difficulty of correcting what they thought was wrong simply by editing. Most of the extract consisted of an interview with Nilsen, and it was the interview that was considered to be wrong:

> *The public had not been served anything from that, absolutely nothing wrong in*

> *producing that for experts, pathologists, if it's an insight into them sort of persons, but what the hell is me, or the public getting from that, I just don't know.*

The programme stated, by way of explaining the inclusion of the Nilsen interview, that it was an important contribution to our understanding of the mind of a serial killer.

The shock that this respondent felt at watching the clip was based on the fact that he could not locate the programme within any context that gave the programme purpose. It appealed only to his curiosity, and that offered weak protection against the horrors which Nilsen described. But what we see, or rather do not see, in this man's reaction is any of the objection to Nilsen exhibited by the female satellite viewers.

What these respondents could not grasp is that Nilsen could be so 'matter of fact' in describing what he did with the bodies of his victims. Respondents were aware that they were watching another world at work and some found it fascinating:

> *I've never seen a film where there's been a murderer like this before, so cool. I suppose in one respect you can get to see what he is really like, whether you should see it or not is down to option again. Do you ban it? I don't think it was such a bad idea putting it on. It's disturbing, but it's very interesting too. I think it's revolting.*

Those who agreed that it was right to transmit the programme, agreed only because of the lateness of the hour that it was shown, 10.45 pm. One viewer said, *'There was enough warning to get rid of your kids, but at the same time the warnings didn't advertise the ... [content]'*. He was unsure whether he would wish a sixteen year old to watch such a programme, an indication of just how 'disturbing' he thought it was. Furthermore, although he agreed that it was good to give a warning about the programme before transmission, in effect he thought that that provided little real protection to the viewer, it was impossible to have predicted the type of material the programme would include. It was not as if the programme could have warned that certain pictures might be shown and that they might upset some viewers. The frightening material was Nilsen's words, and the composure with which he delivered his report.

What we see here are the complexities, once we move beyond the obvious ideas of violence, such as close-up shots of the dead, pictures of blood and injury and so on, that are involved in understanding what it is that shocks and disturbs viewers.

*(c) Women 16–24 years old:* If we now leave the male satellite viewers, and look at the responses of some of the younger respondents, we can begin to trace the boundaries of acceptance of a programme that in itself did not actually depict any scenes of violence. The young women, aged 16–24, did not approve of this clip, but neither did they think it could be edited to make it more acceptable. Specifically asked if they wished to edit any sequence, one woman replied:

> *Not really, it didn't show much detail anyway, as pictures. As far as it went it didn't show anything gruesome, it was just his descriptions and the way he sat so coldly, as if he was reading a script. I suppose it was interesting, but was it necessary?*

Even in this young group we see a challenge to the intent of the programme. If we talk in terms of the acceptance of violence, as opposed to the shock or disturbance that violent images might create, then clearly a central part of acceptance is whether any purpose is served by the material seen or heard. Factual violence could not shelter, as in the case of fictional violence, behind the defence of entertainment.

Even the female satellite viewers did not draw this programme into the realm of entertainment. It was seen as a documentary and therefore had to fulfil the canon of not just presenting information, but presenting information that had a purpose to it; namely, had some intellectual or social relevance to the viewer. This programme was held by many not to have such qualities. *'Is it really necessary that we see the interviews with him, the jury would need such evidence, but we don't'.*

Some members of this group did find the sequence acceptable, but the overall view was that it was not. The main reason for the non-acceptance, apart from those already given, was the character of Nilsen himself. He was loathed: *'He must be sick. He thinks by saying that he had to make himself drunk to cut the bodies up and was sick afterwards, it excuses him'.*

*(d) Men 16–24 years old:* Throughout the series of film clips the young men, aged 16–24, showed themselves to be fairly unmoved by scenes of violence. They criticized programmes because of the way they were shot, but tended not to respond to pictures on the grounds that they were shocked by them. The interview with Nilsen was considered, a *'bit boring'* by one young man. He believed that the programme *'had so many constraints put on it by the government so that nobody would copy cat what this guy had done, it was pretty boring really'.* They wanted more detail, but not detail about what he had done because, *'everybody knew what he was supposed to have done'.* What one of the men wanted was, *'because it was a documentary, more into why he did it, not the details of where the bodies were and how many and what not'.*

Like the young women, they could not see the point of showing viewers what was supposed to be of benefit to a psychiatrist in understanding the mind of a serial killer.

The young men thus showed little ready acceptance of the programme, but, despite the rather trenchant criticism concerning its value, were not sufficiently stirred to agitate for its removal on either a scene basis or as a whole.

*(e) Men 24–35 years old:* The older men were made angry by the programme in a way that was not the case with the younger men.

> *I remember watching when it was on and I just found it appalling, listening to this man talking about dismembering bodies, talking about all the intricacies of doing it. Appalling.*

This man found no reason for showing the interview. His lack of acceptance for screening Nilsen's account of the killings was that he felt that to be taken into Nilsen's world was to threaten the humanity of the viewer. Another man in the group, having worked in a morgue, and *'seen bodies sliced and cut and everything else'*, claimed he was impervious to the sight or discussion of anything to do with dismemberment. Nevertheless, he proved a fierce critic of the programme. It did not fulfil the informative role he expected of a documentary.

> *The programme was about building psychological profiles of serial murderers. The*

*night I watched it I wasn't any more enlightened about how a mass murderer's mind works.*

Had the programme been of some informative value to the viewer, then, as far as these men were concerned, the subject matter itself, and the actual interview with Nilsen, would have been appropriate for a documentary. The fact was, however, that the programme was seen to fail as documentary. These men were not frightened or upset by the programme, it simply made them uneasy that television would present such material.

*(f) Men 40–55 years old:* As we go further up the age range, but remaining with the men, what we see is not just an objection to the programme on the grounds already presented – its pointlessness to this lay audience – but moral outrage that a person such as Nilsen should be allowed to express himself to the public.

> *He's the star of the bloody thing, isn't he – he certainly was behaving like he is. He should have been locked up, forgotten about or topped, end of story. They shouldn't be allowed to boost their own egos by exhibiting in front of others what they've done.*

There can be no doubting this man's anger at the fact that Nilsen was accorded such status, or his annoyance at the fact that, no matter for how short a time, his life was made easier by getting *'out of his cell'*. Television was seen to give privileges to someone who ought not to be privileged. It was the objection to the man, and the objection to what he had done, that made this programme objectionable. It also, according to one man, frightened him but, as we have already seen, there was no point to the fright, either on an entertainment ground, or on educational information grounds. The group was asked, 'did it frighten you?'

> *Yes, absolutely. Psychotic, chilling. He was so matter of fact, and there was no remorse. No concept that he had actually done anything wrong. Just like a normal activity.*

But he went on to say:

> *How do you define fright? I found it chilling. What is frightening is that there are people who to all intents and purposes are absolutely Joe normal, he could live next door to you sort of thing.*

Although these older men may have shared similarities of view with the young men concerning the value of the programme, their reaction to it, in terms of the effect on them, is remarkably different. They did not say, as one young man did, *'Just leave it'*. They thought the programme ought not to have been shown.

These older men were not blasé about the programme in the same way as the young men were. It frightened them. Or perhaps more accurately, the image presented by Nilsen had the power to haunt well after the programme had finished. This 'haunt-ing' did not occur after viewing fictional violence:

> *If there is a parallel to be drawn, the closest thing I've seen to that in fiction would be Anthony Perkins in* Psycho *– it's that kind of psychology. I think thrillers are sort of ten or fifteen minutes after it's finished and you're back to normal. But that's a haunting thing because it's something that has actually happened and the bloke's just sat there, cool as a cucumber talking about it as if it were just normal.*

*(g) Women 55+ years old:* The oldest group of women, those aged fifty-five plus, would have nothing to do with the Nilsen programme:

> *I don't think I wanted to know that really, any of it. Like a horror story. That's the type of programme I do not watch.*

Another woman was no less certain in her views: '*I didn't enjoy it, it shouldn't be shown. I watched it, not to enjoy it but to see why people might do it*'. This woman was not suggesting that she had actually watched the programme at home, but letting us know that she steeled herself to watch it for the purpose of the editing exercises. This was by far the most sensitive group of respondents and we would frequently notice someone turning away from the screen when something they considered gruesome appeared. We asked the woman who said that she had looked at the screen to see why someone would do such things, whether she thought it had been worthwhile.

> *It's degrading that they expect us to want to watch it. They instil it on us, we haven't a choice. Why should we have to watch it?*

We asked this group, 'If you're watching, would it make you feel frightened?' The very idea that they would watch such a programme was unimaginable:

> *I would switch it off as it's so horrible if I knew it was coming on. It's interesting in a way to see how the police work and catch the criminals, but not the details of the crime.*

Although sensitivity to violent images is high in older men, there can be no escaping the fact that women stand in a different relationship to violence in our society than do men, owing to a greater element of personal fear which surfaces in their reactions to certain forms of screen violence.

*(h) Women 40–55 years old:* The response of the 40–55 year old women to the Nilsen interview was strong. Although not manifestly made as uncomfortable as the older women, they nevertheless were passionate about its screening in a way that suggested a deeper reaction than mere revulsion at the type of person Nilsen was:

> *I haven't seen it, I don't think there was any need for that, it's totally unbelievable what he says. I don't honestly believe that there was any reason to make that film. Everybody knows what he'd done years before, so why go and interview him? Why give him air-space? He loved it, you'd think he was talking about going on holiday or something.*

This objection to Nilsen – '*a horrible person*' – is an estimation anyone might wish to make based on an assessment of his character, although mad might be another one. It is interesting that no-one did call him mad or insane. To have referred to Nilsen as mad would have been to reduce the idea of him as horrible. In the interview he appeared to respondents as strange, but also strangely normal. The fact that he was interviewed also helped to normalize him.

When it was put to this woman who had called Nilsen '*horrible*' that the programme was supposed to be of benefit to science, she was as dismissive of this idea as other respondents had been: '*Yes, but we're not scientists, so we don't need to see it.*'

## Crimewatch

### (i) Description of extract

The *Crimewatch* extract shown to the groups was a sequence of about five minutes duration from a dramatic reconstruction of a violent attack on a woman shopkeeper. As well as the reconstruction with actors taking the part of the victim and her attackers, the programme included both an interview with the actual victim herself and a black and white still photograph, taken at the time, of her face which had been cut with a knife during the attack. The actual knife attack was not reconstructed dramatically, but was evoked by the still photo and the testimony of the real victim (only this key section is reproduced here). The transcript ran as follows:

| | |
|---|---|
| 1. CU woman | Please believe me, that's all the money I have, just take it and go. |
| 2. Over shoulder woman to shot of man wearing stocking mask | She's lying. If you don't tell us I'll make you tell us. |
| 3. CU woman as 1 | VO (real victim) I didn't know he had a knife in his hand |
| 4. Synch int. with real victim | and he just sort of cut me on my face and ... on my face, and then on my chin and he held it up at my eye there and said it'll be your eye next and I just sort of felt it give, you know, it was cut |
| 5 B/W still CU of eyes zooms out to show whole face including wounds | right across my eyebrow, you know blood was running in my eyes. It felt terrible at the time, I mean all you can think about is that your face it seems it's going to be all cut to shreds really, |
| 6. Int. with real victim as 4 | and he kept on hitting and I just passed out, I must have just passed out. Then the next thing I do remember then was coming round |
| 7. High angle shot of woman tied to chair, blood on face | and these, there was 2 were arguing. |
| 8. WS two men arguing in shop | – You mad idiot<br>– You shouldn't have been so hard. What are we going to do now?<br>– I had to. The bitch wouldn't tell me where the safe was.<br>– What are you going to do now?<br>– Come on! |

| | |
|---|---|
| 9. Int. with victim as 4,6 | Victim: They must have thought I was dead, that they'd hit me too hard and they'd killed me. I got the impression that that's what they meant, you know they were just trying to find a way of getting rid of me then. |
| 10. Men pull wool down from shelves, tilt down to reveal woman on floor | Come on! |
| 11. CU match being lit | natural sound |
| 12. Burning newspaper put to wool | |
| 13–17. Five further CU shots of burning wool | |
| 18. Door opening woman crawling out, smoke apparent | |

## (ii) Initial response and editing

All groups could see the public service point of *Crimewatch* and even when they found the event reconstructed to be personally disturbing (*'sickening'* 40–55 year old women), they accepted that the violence portrayed, described or evoked in such reconstructions, was necessary to aid the primary purpose of catching criminals.

The only edits were by the 25–34 year old men who wanted a more horrific colour close-up of the victim's wounds in order to bring home the full horror of the assault. This group also thought that it was more likely that someone would be shocked into turning the criminals in if the victim's testimony was removed and replaced by a strongly worded, scripted description of the knife attack, spoken by the actress.

All groups displayed a high degree of media literacy when it came to *Crimewatch*, recognizing its style of reconstruction instantly. This recognition depended for the most part on the quality of the acting. Phrases like *'bad B movie'* and *'school play'* were used, but these judgements were not as dismissive as they might at first sound. Respondents understood the style and the purpose of the programme. In a sense they were saying that *Crimewatch* reconstructions had to look recognisably different from fictional violence if they were to do their job. Once again a context was provided which made screen violence (and indifferent acting) acceptable.

## (iii) Further responses

(a) Women 16–24 years old: The young women, after been shown *Crimewatch*, and having examined the stills from the programme, said:

> It's [violence] not been shown for entertainment. It's presented for a reason, in order to catch people who commit the crimes, and because that's the reason behind it, that's O.K.

Although many similar comments were made, it is nevertheless worthwhile, in order to understand further how respondents reacted to violence in factual programmes, to examine the reasoning behind the general acceptance.

Because the programme was not *'for entertainment'*, but for the purpose of appre-hending criminals, the above woman found it easy to accept the picture of the cut and battered face of a woman who had been robbed, tied up and an attempt made on her life by setting fire to the shop she ran. What also made the images shown acceptable was the fact that the programme showed pictures of her after she had recovered: *'She's all right now. Her face has healed, though we're aware she's been left mentally scarred'.*

We asked this group, given that they considered the point of the programme was to jog people's memories and have viewers come forward to volunteer information to the police, whether or not the programme ought to be more graphic than it was:

> *It's not necessary [to be more graphic], we know the details of what they did to her from what she told us.*

(b) Men 16–24 years old: The men of the same age as the above women also found the violence portrayed in *Crimewatch* acceptable, although they did tend to be more critical of the programme. One or two considered that it erred on the side of the sensational in, for example, the topics that it took for inclusion:

> *It's always violent crimes that you see, you don't see car thieves on* Crimewatch, *or computer fraud, they have to show stuff (a) that they can't solve, or (b) that is violent, because nobody's gonna watch it otherwise – it's sensationalism again.*

Despite the fact that *Crimewatch* was criticized for pursuing viewers through sensa-tionalism, it was never as heavily criticized as *Cops* had been. These men also saw *Crimewatch* as performing a civic function, indeed they saw that aspect of the programme overriding the populist element in the programme.

> *The whole point of the thing is that they are trying to get members of the public to ring in and identify the criminals. Now if all you ever get is one still photo of the woman and you don't hear it all, then it doesn't generate as much sympathy, does it?*

The idea of using the technique of dramatic reconstruction to assist the police was approved of, but some of the men in this group, although they recognized the genre easily enough, were confused by pictures of the real life victim talking and the actress taking the role of the victim. As one man said: *'Was she playing herself? There were shots that were obviously her, but the likeness to her, the actress playing her looks very like her'.*

When the group was asked how they could tell it was a reconstruction, the reply was:

> *The voice-over all the way through. They all seem to do that. At the start there's always someone who says, 'Oh I knew they were shifty the first time I saw them', they could have been half a mile away. It's got to be reconstructed, you just don't have cameras down these places.*

(c) Women 25–34 years old: The 25–34 year old women, although all agreeing that there could be no mistake that *Crimewatch* was a reconstruction, did concede that certain scenes might well be accepted as fictional drama:

> *When it showed the shop and she sat in the back, she could hear them shouting, that*

> *little shot it could have been* The Bill *or something, but when you hear the voice-over and she said, 'Oh dear' and you could hear them arguing, then you realized.*

This group of women did not think the violence in *Crimewatch* was distressing, or at least, *'no more distressing than listening to the news'*. The difference between the news, however, and a reconstruction, is that the latter, because it has similarities to fictional drama in that it focuses on the individual as a person has the potential for creating an empathy missing in the news. The characters are not, however, as fully drawn as they are in fiction and hence the degree of emotional development between the viewer and actor/victim is limited. Nevertheless, one woman did say, *'I don't think this [reconstruction] is more distressing [than the news] it makes you see her as a human being, so you are more likely to shop somebody'*.

*(d) Women 40–55 years old:* It is quite clear that the younger respondents were not disturbed by the violence shown. Some of the older respondents, however, although they approved of the programme, were less sanguine about the violence. When the group of women aged 40–55 were asked if they would wish to edit anything from the programme, one viewer replied:

> *I'd rather you didn't take anything out, quite honestly. It disturbs you to think that it actually happened to start with. It frightened me when they set fire to the shop, that was a bit of a shock. But it had to be shown, you can't cut anything out.*

We asked her, showing her the still photograph of the injured victim, if it should be removed. She thought not, *'because people seeing that, if they saw that, and they knew anybody, surely they would come forward'*.

The difference in judgement probably stems from the respondent's greater fear of crime than that of the young men, and her greater personal desire to see criminals caught. The women in this group showed a great sensitivity to lawlessness. In discussing whether programmes such as *Crimewatch* created a fear that similar crimes might happen to them, one woman said:

> *You're not safe anywhere these days, you don't trust anybody. If you're in your car you lock your door when you get to certain areas. I lock it at night, especially coming home, I lock that door. And if I should forget, which I rarely do, and when I'm pulling up to a traffic light I say, 'oh my door'. I used to take my dog for a walk in the wood and fields and I don't now.*

We can see from these comments why it should be that the violence in *Crimewatch* would be more frightening for these women than it was for the younger men. It had a reality to it that it did not possess for the young men. The reconstruction shown in *Crimewatch* reflected these women's everyday reality, and that reality was made up of fears, as well as actual happenings. Hence, *Crimewatch*, in capturing the real world of this viewer, was bound to make the violence of these sequences of greater impact to her than it was for any of the young men.

It would be wrong to say that *Crimewatch* was responsible for the fear, or in any direct sense that it increased the fear these women had of crime. The programme frightened them, but more in the manner of reminding them of the unruliness of modern-day life than implanting fundamental worries.

Because this group of women were wary about crime, and *Crimewatch* appeared to reinforce this wariness, we wished to know how far the programme ought to proceed in reconstructing the various sequences of the crime. Asked if the programme should have shown the actual beating that the shop owner received, rather than simply mentioning the fact, the response was one of agreement with the programme in not showing the actual beating: *'Tied, yes. To get it across, horror, panic, to show what had happened, without actually seeing her being beaten'*. This woman said it would have made her more angry with the criminals had she seen the actual beating: *'I think it would have made me more angry, but I don't think you could bear to watch her being beaten up'*.

The difference between this group and both the younger groups that have been examined was that these women appeared to be much more engaged in the programme. It was this engagement, or rather the reasons for the engagement, that made them sensitive to the violence. Although this age group feared becoming a victim of crime, it was also the case, as with many older people, that crime stood as a metaphor for all that was wrong with the modern world – a world that, to them, had got worse since their youth.

Often the older respondents would hark back to when one could walk the streets without fear of being attacked or leave one's door open without offering an invitation to burglary. Objectively, they could be right, but only in the sense, at least with regard to physical violence, that violence used to be more restricted to known rough quarters of a town. The difference now is – and this is supported by other research carried out at the Institute – that householders in 'respectable' areas no longer feel protected against violence: it is the migration of violence that most classically separates the period of these people's youth and the present, not the absolute level of violence.

*(e) Women 55+ years old:* If we now turn to the oldest age groups in our sample, and their reaction to *Crimewatch*, we will see that they were the most emotionally moved by the violence shown.

After showing *Crimewatch*, the over fifty-five women were asked, 'what are your reactions to that?' The first comment was, *'Anger ... because of what they did to her, it makes you angry and you feel like retaliating'*. Her anger was obvious, but the supplementary question was put to her, 'Did it upset you?' She replied, *'Yes it did, she had no way of defending herself'*. She justified the programme, however, by saying, *'But it's factual and I think we ought to know what's going on'*. The rest of the group were asked what they thought was the 'point or purpose of *Crimewatch*': *'To see if anyone has seen anything, they do get results, but that was a bit ... '*

The suggestion of this viewer was that perhaps *Crimewatch* had over-stepped the mark of acceptability, even though the violence shown was intended to help catch those who had been responsible for the violence. When specifically asked did she think they showed too much violence, she replied, *'I think they did'*. Although this group was shocked by what they saw, they did not wish to make any edits.

The impact of living alone on the reception of violent images was explored fully with this group. One woman was asked, 'what difference does it make if you are on your own watching, is it worse watching on your own?' She had already mentioned that television upset her if the violence shown was too graphic and in directly answering our question said, *'Yes [it upsets], I turn it off, I'd rather not watch'*. For older people, living alone amplifies their sensitivity to violence and suffering. As this woman explained:

> When you are on your own you don't have anyone to discuss it with and so you take it in and worry about it. We also worry someone might come to the house. It's just disturbing that things like that happen.

Watching alone, so that images or descriptions in programmes have little chance of being exorcized or displaced in discussions with others, provides, when allied with feelings of physical vulnerability, a strong basis for extreme sensitivity to portrayals of factual violence.

Not surprisingly, no one in this group considered that the images of violence ought to be strengthened. One woman said:

> We were told how she looked at the time, and I think that is quite enough. The good thing about this was she was telling the story and we knew she'd turned out alright, apart from the mental scars.

By allowing the victim to speak for herself, absolute proof was given that she had at least physically recovered from her ordeal. Without her appearance this episode of *Crimewatch* would have been much more upsetting than it actually was. Her appearance helped 'close' the narrative and provided the viewer with a 'certainty' that might otherwise have been missing. By certainty we mean that the viewer is not left wondering what happened, or left to imagine what might be the case. It was helped by having the victim, whose face had considerably healed, appear before any pictures of her damaged face were shown. Thus, as far as this woman was concerned, a double 'certainty' was brought into operation: certainty by the positioning and certainty of the ending. The fact that this group of over 55 year old women, some of whom lived alone, mentioned that they drew comfort from the victim's appearance, was a clear demonstration of how sensitive they were to the portrayal of real life violence through dramatic reconstruction.

## World in Action

### (i) Description of the extract

Respondents were shown another dramatic reconstruction, this time from a *World in Action* programme about a convicted criminal referred to as Dennis the Menace. This piece was shot in a quite stylized manner. Slow motion was used, as was soft focus and images were superimposed on each other. There was an elaborate sound track both of the events that were happening and of the victim's response. The reconstruction told the story of a man who was tied up in his own flat, raped, tortured and nearly drowned in his own bath. Respondents did not see the actual events for the most part, although at one time there was a fleeting shot of a man being pushed under water in an attempt to drown him. The style in which the reconstruction was shot was the very opposite of *cinema verité*. It was highly crafted both in terms of sound and vision, furthermore the word 'reconstruction' was visible in the top left-hand corner of the frame throughout the sequence.

The victim and the offender were seen walking together along a walkway in a council estate. They appeared to be joking and engaged in mock fisticuffs. The victim-to-be was clearly subservient. This three-shot section was followed by an interview with the neighbour of the victim. Three highly stylized shots then followed evoking the whipping. The neighbour reappeared, speaking as before, but describing the sexual attack. This was followed by a shot of the victim's head being held under water and then by the victim jumping or being pushed through a glass panel in a door. The transcript went as follows:

| | |
|---|---|
| 1. Medium close-up (MCU) of man walking along | V.O: The year is 1982. Dennis Wilkinson is about to commit a sickening crime, so serious |
| 2. Wide shot of two men, including 1, on council estate walkway | he will face the prospect of life imprisonment. For pure sadistic pleasure he's about to turn on a man who thought he was his friend. |
| 3. MCU of second man, matching shot 1 | We'll call his victim Joe Perrera. His neighbours remember Joe as a trusting, vulnerable man. |
| 4. Synch int. with neighbour | Int: He was kind. No doubt about that, he was a very kind person. He was religious, hence that's how we come to talk, you know, we got into a conversation over religion. |
| 5. As 1 slow<br>mix to: | V.O: Dennis robbed Joe of almost everything he owned. |
| 6. CU hand putting glass down on table and picking up belt<br>slow mix to: | Then after a drinking session he took the cruellest pleasure in torturing him. |
| 7. CU of face of man clearly whipping someone, belt is not in shot<br>superimposed over: | With another man he kept Joe prisoner in his own flat. |
| 8. CU, back of victim's head, lying on bed (7 superimposed throughout) | For a day and a night they brutally sexually abused him. |
| 9. As shot 7 | They inflicted over 120 separate injuries and rubbed salt and hair shampoo into his wounds.<br>Neighbour as VO: The two lads in the flat with him and they had him tied up in the bathroom |

| | |
|---|---|
| 10. Synch int. with neighbour as 4 | Synch Int. neighbour: and they'd also had him tied to the bed. They'd raped him and they'd been whipping him with wire whilst he was tied to the bed. |
| 11. CU head being held under water mix to: | V.O: After all this Dennis Wilkinson almost drowned |
| 12. CU over shoulder of man attempting drowning mix to: | Joe in his own bath. Joe thought he was going to die. |
| 13. CU body breaking through glass mix to: | (pause, sound of glass breaking and man moaning) |
| 14. WS of body breaking through glass | In desperation he plunged through a glass door to escape. He fled to his friend's house. |

*(ii) Initial response and editing*

The 16–24 year old men were happy with the reconstruction, but were in a definite minority as far as this film was concerned, which became the most re-edited piece of all the selections.

The 40–55 year old women thought it *'terrible,' 'horrible'*. They particularly objected to the words 'sexual abuse' in the voice-over, much of which they thought was particularly upsetting. At the very end of the sequence, there was the sound of breaking glass, followed by a shot (13) of a person or body crashing through the glass panel in a door. For a brief moment there was no explanation until the voice-over explained that the victim had gone through the window in order to escape. These respondents were distressed by not knowing what had happened and had assumed that the shot indicated his dead body being thrown out of the flat. In the editing they asked if the sequence could be re-edited so that the voice-over description and the pictures in this section were synchronous, thereby explaining more clearly what had happened. In effect they were objecting to a common industry practice of 'leading with the sound,' whereby the sound of a new sequence precedes the incoming picture. They wanted it made clear that the man who was being tortured was escaping. There was no longer any doubt as to what was happening. The positive truth of the victim's escape was instantly apparent, instead of being withheld for even a split second.

The technique of 'leading with the sound' does not in itself automatically create a disorientating effect. The testimony of the real victim is introduced into the *Crime-watch* reconstruction by this very same technique and, there, the transition was accomplished with the audience certain of what was going on.

Fictional narrative may depend for some of its effect on withholding information, indeed suspense has been defined as 'an anxious uncertainty about what is going to happen, especially to those characters with whom we have established bonds of sympathy'[1]. The narrative drive of information programming is normally quite the contrary. News editors and documentary directors do not include the creation of suspense in their professional repertoire. *Crimewatch* originated in the BBC's Current Affairs department and the style of the series is one very much rooted in this factual tradition. Respondents recognized this and made allowances for it. They claimed they could come into the room during transmission and instantly recognize that the programme was *Crimewatch*. The Dennis the Menace reconstruction, although part of a current affairs programme, was shot in a manner hardly typical of the normal run of *World in Action*. It made use of techniques more reminiscent of fictional production.

Sympathy with the victim was also a factor in the audience's response. The opening three shots of the reconstruction established both characters with 'Joe,' the victim of violence, seen as being both innocent and vulnerable. Unlike the victim in the nightclub brawl who was deemed to be capable of looking after himself, he attracted unalloyed sympathy from the respondents.

As far as the 25–34 year old men were concerned the piece was pure sensationalism. One person particularly felt that the sound effects were distasteful. They wanted to take out the beating sequence and the drowning shot. Their version just used the neighbour's testimony and a few general shots to set up the sequence. In effect they cut the final half of the piece and the detailed sound effects.

The 25–34 year old female group equally found the voice-over upsetting. They felt sorry for the victim and they were upset by the evocation of sexual abuse and the details of putting salt and shampoo in his wounds. When asked if they would edit the material, they wanted to take out the drowning, the tying up and the beating sequence, certainly if it was transmitted earlier than 9 o'clock. The version thus produced was exactly the same as the 25–34 year old men.

One man in the 40–55 year old male group said the piece made his hair stand on end. Like the other groups he found the last four shots (11, 12, 13 and 14) disturbing and he would have particularly taken out the drowning shot (11).

This group thought there was less point in this particular extract than in the Nilsen piece. The man who said it made his hair stand on end had seen the programme on transmission and remembered it. All the group said it should have been transmitted after the Watershed. Somebody said it might have been better just to describe the actual events. There was also a comment that the actual reconstruction sequence with the superimposition, slow motion, soft focus and sound effects was more like drama and they found this made it more chilling. They thought it would have been equally disturbing if it had been in the context of a fictional programme, simply because of the particular nastiness of the abuse and torture.

The 16–24 year old female group was mixed in its response. One member wanted to keep the piece as it was, while another person thought it acceptable except for the crying on the sound track. A third thought there was no need for the reconstruction, feeling the story could have been told with the voice-over, the testament of the

---

1   M.H. Abrams, 1965. *A glossary of literary terms* 1957. Nolt, Rinehart and Winston, New York.

neighbour and by leaving the viewer's imagination to do the work. One woman said she wanted the drowning shot (11) to be removed while another two actually created the same version as the older women by 'pulling up' the voice-over explanation to coincide with the picture of the body crashing through the glass (13). Three saw no point in the piece at all and felt there was too much detail. They found 'rape' a powerful word whether used towards a man or towards a woman, more powerful certainly than the phrase 'sexual abuse'.

The 55+ year old men thought that the reconstruction was *'horrendous'*, *'terrible'*, *'too violent'*, *'sickening'*. *'What's the purpose?'* they said. One said *'it's the worst we've seen because everything is in the mind'*. Another just said *'where's the off button?'* One man said he did not want to see it at all; he thought it was awful and that it had no purpose. When asked how they would edit the sequence, this group cut out all the shots depicting the torture (from 5 onwards) simply using the two pieces of interview from the neighbour to tell the story. Two of them completely missed the word 'reconstruction' which was on the screen all the way through, claiming they were watching the action and did not see the key word. The 55+ women cut the two shots of the drowning sequence in the bath (11, 12).

The male satellite viewers found this edition of *World in Action* 'horrific', *'not really necessary'* and felt *'it went too far'*. Again, some thought the voice-over was sufficient. One man found it disturbing precisely because it played on the imagination. While the sequence was not explicit, it made the respondents use their imagination and was as a result more upsetting. As in other groups, one person failed to notice the fact that *Reconstruction* was written on the screen throughout. Some objected to the use of slow motion and elaborate sound effects and said they made it more like drama. They felt that these recognisably higher production qualities added to its effect. These male satellite viewers did not edit any of the pieces offered them, but insisted that the programme be transmitted after the Watershed.

The female satellite viewers thought the film was violent and they were shocked. They did not like the sound effects, particularly the simulated voice of the victim groaning and crying. They knew it was a reconstruction because they saw the words on the screen, but also because there was no dialogue. The word 'rape' shocked them and it was more shocking, they said, for a man to be raped. Some of them would have cut out the sound effects and the whipping, yet half the group would leave it as it was. These women did not think it was entertaining in any way, but they thought it should be shown to shock. Although the majority of the group would have left the sequence as it was, there was a caveat that it should not have been shown pre-Watershed. They too demanded context: What else had he done? Where did this happen?

*(iii) Further responses*

To understand the reactions to *World in Action*, it is helpful to compare it with *Crimewatch* which, because of its supposed central purpose of assisting the police and the lack of close re-enactment of violence, met with general approval from the groups. The discussion of *Crimewatch* did indicate that the dramatic reconstruction of actual events has a special power to disturb, particularly in the case of older respondents who lived alone. The fact that such violence had actually occurred, and in mundane settings, carried the message that what had happened to the person on screen could conceivably happen to them.

At the end of each programme the presenter, Nick Ross, makes a statement to reassure viewers that the chances of them being a victim of crime are slim. This shows that the programme itself recognizes that it has a responsibility not to alarm viewers unnecessarily. As we have seen, the programme, within reason, did not unduly alarm viewers by the amount of violence shown.

The reconstruction shown in *World in Action* could hardly be said to feature the mundane world. The programme dealt with a 'supergrass' who had given evidence against a number of people, who were duly convicted of crimes, in return for a reduction in his own sentence. The supergrass was later found to be lying, and the programme, through reconstruction, set out to show his true nature.

This reconstruction shocked respondents far more than *Crimewatch* did, and from some met with disapproval. Even among those who approved of the programme, some considered that to edit certain sequences was in order. Thus, one can have reconstructed violence which is removed from the individual's own world in the sense that the possibility of it happening to them is remote – this was the world of the criminal supergrass – but it shocks more than reconstructed violence close to the viewer's own world – the friendly little shop that exists in every provincial town.

*(a) Women 55+ years old:* The *World in Action* reconstruction was liberal in its use of dramatic effect. After the women aged fifty-five and over had finished viewing the clip, they were asked what they thought of it, to which one woman said: '*Horrible, horrific*'. The programme went out at 8.30 pm, and we asked the group, in light of such a response, if they thought it was too early a time for such a broadcast. It was agreed that it was, but some even went so far as to say it should not have been shown at all: '*They shouldn't show it as there's not much point, they are not appealing to witnesses like Crimewatch does. If they do have to show it, it should be on much later*'.

These women all agreed that the violence was more shocking than the violence seen in *Crimewatch*: '*(It) is a softer programme, that. To me that's violence*'. The point to stress is the simple one that, had the manner in which *World in Action* reconstructed the violence of its programme been applied to *Crimewatch*, the shock would have been so much worse than that experienced in watching *World in Action*. Their reaction to a similar level of violent portrayal in *Crimewatch* would have been one of deep worry, not just repulsion.

*(b) Men 55+ years old:* The men over fifty-five, although not as sensitive as the women to watching the *World in Action* sequence, were nevertheless highly critical of it. One man, although he agreed, '*you have got to face these things happen*', doubted that viewers in his age group were as comfortable with such material as younger viewers:

> *If we were under thirty, all young men, swingers, just married or whatever ... life has changed a tremendous amount in thirty years. Maybe younger people could see this, but for me I can't, it just sickens me. It's an age thing maybe, a younger age group could see it.*

The group was asked, if they had just walked into their living room, could they tell what type of programme it was. Might it be that they could be confused into thinking they were watching a play? Some thought they could have been and particularly referred to the shot, *'where he dived through the window'*.

Throughout the reconstruction, every frame showed the word 'reconstruction' but most missed the information:

> *I missed that completely. No, I never noticed it. I noticed in the first few [frames] but when the action started you start watching something else.*

At the very moment, then, when the warning was needed that the scene shown was a reconstruction, the respondent had focused concentration on to the action itself and had failed to note what had in effect become background material. This group wished for quite severe editing, taking out the noise of the victim, pulling the voice-over describing his escape in advance of his crashing through the window and giving a bigger role to the account of the neighbour. After showing the re-cut version of the sequence one respondent said: *'I don't mind now, but I don't want to see the rest. The guy getting away like that is acceptable to me but the rest isn't'*.

Without the editing the feeling of this group was captured by the comment of one man:

> *It is a queer phenomenon – why they have to make this stuff I can't understand. It just baffles me; not what they are thinking, but what they are aiming at. To get the ratings up?*

All agreed that if such a programme was shown, then it had to be for *'late night viewing that sort of thing'*. *'Very late, twelve o'clock for insomniacs'*.

Throughout the course of the discussions, respondents of all age groups believed ratings played a part in the decisions that television companies make in deciding what to show. But what is also clear is that when something was thought to have been included on these grounds, it was condemned for its lack of authenticity. Such a sequence was not considered essential for the point that the programme wished to make. In this group's opinion, violence was included in the *World in Action* programme to grab attention through excitement and thus increase its appeal.

*(c) Female satellite viewers:* If we turn now to the female satellite viewers, it would appear that factual violence was not that much of an attraction, in this particular programme. The women felt sorry for the victim, who was presented as a not over-bright, but amiable and trusting, person: *'I think what shocks you more is it's his friend, he's done it to his friend, his pal'*.

The ability of this violence to shock appeared to be based, independent of the horrors of the attack, on the fact that a rule of human relationships was broken – one should not turn on friends in the manner portrayed in this film. This fact alone was enough to make the violence in the sequence shown especially shocking, and probably carried a greater power to disturb than had it been two criminals falling out with each other. The other factor that may have made this violence less appealing to the women was that the victim of the attack, as well as being tortured, was raped. These women were sensitive, as indeed all the women were, to the portrayal of rape.

Most of the women in the group thought that the reconstruction in this *World in*

*Action* programme was too violent: '*It was too violent by far, the poor bloke getting drowned*'. Those in the group who had seen *Fatal Attraction* had mentioned how much they had enjoyed the film, and mentioned spontaneously the bath scene in it when discussing the attempted drowning in this programme. The researchers put to them that, '*Fatal Attraction* was much more violent than this', and registered disbelief that they really were shocked by the violence in this reconstruction:

> Fatal Attraction *happened in America and I think with the voice-over you realize this is something that has happened, it's not a picture on telly. Also it's not a normal thing to happen, they raped him and kept him prisoner, and they whipped him, they didn't just actually beat him up and leave him, or even just keep him prisoner. The things that he did to him makes it more ghastly.*

The women wished to edit the pictures of the victim being whipped and especially the sounds of him groaning: '*He's making noises, it's actually showing you the violence there, the visual violence is more upsetting than just saying, 'and he whipped him'*. There was not, however, total consensus in this group. Some resisted the idea of any editing, and in doing so exhibited that trait mentioned earlier, their pleasure in entertainment which revolved around excitement:

> *I wouldn't take nothing out because it's there to shock. It happened and they're showing what has happened. You've got the on/off switch. If you don't want to watch it you turn it off.*

Her further comments showed that the manner in which she watched this reconstruction had close affinities to watching pure entertainment drama:

> *I think with all these if you know what happens afterwards, and whether owt's happened to him, or if he got away with it, it makes you think differently about the film anyway.*

It did seem, even though this group said there was no confusion in their minds that what they had watched was a reconstruction, that this woman viewed the programme as she would view fictional drama. She enjoyed the clip and part of that enjoyment, one suspects, was that she pulled it in the direction of fictional drama.

*(d) Male satellite viewers:* The male satellite viewers did not think the programme was good in the manner of some of their female counterparts. '*Horrific to say the least*', was the reaction of one man, accompanied by surprise that the programme had gone out before the Watershed. This group made great issue about the time of its transmission; '*I think you've got a Watershed, why not use it?*'

As a whole, these men were reluctant to make cuts in the programme. They could not see the point of the programme, unlike some of the female satellite viewers, for whom the point was in the excitement of the dramatic reconstruction of the violence.

> *I think it's back to the same again, straightforward viewing figures only ... We haven't gained anything by watching that. Why do we need to know that [detail of the violence]? If they were after evidence to nail that guy I could well understand the programme, nothing wrong with that at all.*

Comparison with *Crimewatch* was made. The major difference that this group saw between the two reconstructions was the use of dramatic effect. Indeed, this sequence was seen as more drama than documentary, and for that reason was condemned, or at least not especially approved of in terms of its social value.

It was agreed that *'it is certainly more likely to confuse than Crimewatch'*. And the reason:

> *It was very realistic, the* World in Action *one. I think the quality of the production makes it better anyway. They are using television effects to get the best out of the crime basically.*

*World in Action* generally, but not this particular offering, was described as a *'class programme'*. The very 'class' of the *World in Action* team had, however, by their skill, transformed a reconstruction into a drama. Production values did not always need to be high for a programme to work its message, and if too high in dramatic reconstruction so that the drama was over-played, the message might have been in danger of being lost as the drama took over to collapse the point of the document.

Judging by the comments made in the case of this programme, it was the inclusion of violence for dramatic effect that puzzled the respondent.

*(e) Women 40–55 years old:* The women, aged 40–55, after watching the *World in Action* programme, described the reconstruction as horrible. In the words of one woman:

> *That was terrible. Sexual abuse, the rough stuff, but it was the sexual abuse I think more than anything. I think it was absolutely terrible. Mind you, you still didn't see anything, did you, but there again, he was telling you.*

Once more we see the power of words to disturb the viewer. It was true that the rape scene was not at all clear. But the voice-over made the viewer aware that at some point in the proceedings he was raped.

A debate took place within this group about what they found the most disturbing, the visuals or the voice-over and sound effects. Three of the group considered the visuals to be the most disturbing. However, as one woman said, to general agreement:

> *I think they were equal. I think it was hearing what they were saying and seeing it was just the same. What he must have gone through, poor fellow, he couldn't have known when they started if he was gonna live or die, would he, before they put his head under the water.*

What we see here, no doubt the reason why this programme unsettled the respondents so much, was that an element of empathy with the victim had developed, indicated by words such as *'poor fellow'*. The programme painted a sympathetic picture of the victim. His friend, to whom he had staggered for help, described how Joe was gentle, well-liked in the neighbourhood and a religious man.

It was not surprising that certain respondents would find this portrayal of a gentle giant appealing. It was not a reconstruction of actuality for it was too finely drawn. It was more a case of the setting of the scene for a dramatic happening. When the respondent followed Joe into his torture, it was not surprising that it had a most powerful impact. He had been established as a real person. He was not, as with the victims in *Crimewatch*, a figure around which a point was to be made.

It was mentioned previously that the impact of violence in factual programmes depended to some extent on the victim. Joe's status was established as a *'nice guy'*. The only difference between this and fiction was that the respondents knew that Joe was a real person, and the shock caused by the crash of glass and a flying body was that they did not know whether or not this real person was a dead person.

This group very purposefully began to edit the scene in an attempt to make it more acceptable by removing the suspense. This they did by pulling the voice-over back, as described above.

Following this editing, the programme was shown again. All now agreed that this was much better and acceptable: *'I think it's better now how it's done'. 'It's the words that make all the difference, best before you see it happening'.*

*(f) Men 40–55 years old:* The establishment of 'certainty' relieved the programme of some of its horror, particularly so for the women, and most of the men in the 40–55 age group showed similar sentiments. They did not however demand the close editing requested by the women. The programme bothered them. One man said:

> It's just that one human being can do that to another, it's beyond me. The guy [victim] was a very nice religious ... nice pleasant fellow who'd do anything for you.

Through the invention of scenes rather than the reconstructing of scenes, the building of characters instead of simply portraying figures, the violent imagery was amplified to a point where it disturbed some respondents.

*(g) Men 16–24 years old:* The young men, aged 16–24, differed from the age groups covered so far in their response to the programme. One viewer even considered that *'It was quite tastefully done, you didn't actually see anything. It was all shot in slow motion, you got the picture'.* Of all the groups, these young men appeared to be the least likely to be shocked.

Real life happens in real time, and not in slow motion, and it was interesting therefore that the dramatic technique of slowing the action down to provide an elongation of the most tense moments was considered tasteful. Although one cannot be certain about such matters, the grammar for understanding reality which these young men applied to television was different from that applied by older respondents. There was sufficient in the comments which they made about the *World in Action* reconstruction to suggest that this may well be true, and provide understanding as to why they differed from most of the other groups in concluding that not only was the manner in which the violence portrayed acceptable, but was also *'tasteful'*.

> *The acts that were being described was far worse than the acts that were visually seen. I don't think there would have been any words to be able to describe what went on, or have what went on actually shown on television.*

They were asked if they would remove any of the voice reports from the reconstruction:

> *No, I don't think so. It was more objective than that one we heard from TVS. That was peanuts to what this guy had done to the other bloke, and yet if you compare the two the one from TVS sounds much worse. I think that it's interesting that the level*

*of violence [World in Action] is worse than the TVS one, but TVS made it sound worse. This keeps to the facts exactly.*

What we have here, and this was not a contradiction of the above, was an admission that words could conjure up images, but also implied was the belief that facts must be shown and it did so because it visually took the viewer through the story.

For these young men *World in Action* did not dramatize the story and thus add to its shock value, but through dramatic technique made the account objective. It would certainly appear that the manner in which these respondents comprehended the world was well-fitted to a dramatic reconstruction that used cinematic techniques to portray factual events. In short, there was little that interfered with their acceptance of the programme. This was not the case, as we have seen, with the older groups.

*(h) Women 16–24 years old:* The young women of the same age-group, exposed to similar training in the appreciation of imagery, might be expected to react in the same way. In fact, their reaction differed.

They did not like the manner in which *World in Action* reconstructed the story of the supergrass. They showed themselves sensitive to the violence, and no small part of that was because Joe had been raped. Indeed, although rape could be considered a special case of violence, what all violence of a factual type appeared to capture was the feeling of vulnerability of many women.

Some of the women in this group had seen the film, *Silence of the Lambs*, and were asked if they would watch that on their own: *'Not really, we had to look away a few times'*. The imprisonment and torment inflicted on a woman in the film might well bother many women, but when asked if the film was more disturbing than *Crimewatch*, one young woman said:

> *Crimewatch is more disturbing, because they show the way criminals break into the houses and you think it might be yours.*

In the case of the reconstruction, it was not that they considered the situation that Joe found himself in would be visited on them, but that the violence was real. It actually happened and thus carried unpleasant reminders of their own vulnerability.

Despite the fact that these women made a great distinction about the levels of violence appropriate in factual compared with fictional programmes, the manner in which the reconstruction was discussed did have elements of following a fictional drama – they had clearly become involved with the characters and how the story was unfolding. What appeared to stop acceptance/enjoyment of the violence was the knowledge that Joe was a real person. Like respondents in some of the other groups, they would therefore have preferred to follow the sequence of events as they actually happened rather than, as might be the case with fiction, having the story run ahead of itself by presenting the drama first (crashing through a window) and then narrating what happened. One respondent, referring to this sequence, said, *'it was quite confusing'*, which presumably is not the intention of a reconstruction, but might well be the point of a fictional drama.

They did not deny that the facts of the case had to be given, nor did they wish to dodge the brutality of what had occurred.

*(i) Women 25–34 years old:* The women in the next age group, 25–34, were not as sensitive to the violence as the younger women. Certainly they were of an age at which one might expect a certain confidence in dealing with the world. They were married, had children, but were still young. For these women, it was the words that seemed to have the greatest impact:

> *The voice-over. Salt and shampoo rubbed into his wounds, that made me cringe. It's bad enough when you get salt into a little cut on your finger or whatever.*

Despite the fact that the thought of what salt and shampoo rubbed into serious wounds might have felt like, she responded when asked if the words ought to be edited out, *'Definitely leave it in'.* One woman's reaction, although perhaps not capturing entirely the feeling of the group, was, *'It is interesting, I would have watched that. I wanted to see more'.*

The idea of wishing to 'see more', by which she meant more of the story, not more detail, suggested that the drama of the reconstruction was more in her mind when watching the programme than the simple recounting of what had gone on. Someone else observed that it was *'a documentary'.* The question was then put, 'what makes a documentary different from a reconstruction?'

> *Because it [a documentary] was giving you additional information, he had his friend saying he was a kind guy, trusting and what have you.*

When talking about the *World in Action* programme several references were made to *Crimewatch:* *'On Crimewatch they don't show you as much detail, do they?'* It was also pointed out, *'On Crimewatch you wouldn't have seen him in the bath getting pushed under or anything like that'.*

Although this group of women were reasonably unmoved by the violence, they nevertheless wished to question its appropriateness for a pre-Watershed scheduling. They had children: *'It was quite early for the drowning',* commented one woman. Another judgement was: *'I would take the whole filming of that out if it was at 8.30 pm'.*

The discussion of the rape scene provided an example of the distinct sensitivities to specific acts of violence. In general, these respondents were not disturbed by the violence but they were unsettled by the act of rape, and particularly so because the rape was of one man by another. The women agreed that the term, 'sexually abused', the one used in the voice-over, did not strike the same chord as the use of the word 'rape'.

> *Especially man to man sexual abuse. I'm not saying it's right having a man rape a woman, but definitely a man raping a man. It's because you don't hear much of it, it's normally a man raping a woman.*

*(j) Men 25–34 years old:* Moving to the same age group of men, we saw that it was not the violence that disturbed them, but that they brought critical faculties to bear on the programme which condemned the violence. They were not bothered in any personal sense but, and here they were unlike their female counterparts, they considered the violence intellectually to be in bad taste. They could see little valid point for it.

> *The noises had an impact, it was like crying, a whimpering noise – that was a bit*

*distasteful. A lot of the scenes I found shouldn't have been shown. It wants to be more of a factual thing, rather than this is what we think happened and then making a reconstruction of it.*

There is no suggestion here that these men were upset by the violence they saw. In fact, as one of them observed, he would have been prepared to see the violence if the programme had genuine film of the events happening. He objected to them making a reconstruction out of what was thought to have happened. It was the dramatic element in the reconstruction that was considered wrong. One man noted and objected to the elaborate sound track that accompanied the drowning scene.

It would be wrong to conclude that these male respondents were not bothered by the rape of Joe, but it is true to say that they were not disturbed by it. This is a classic case of what has been argued throughout: that to understand the impact of images and words it is necessary to know what those images and words represent to the individual viewer. It is not sufficient to score formulistically some act or scene on a violence scale.

## Violence in the News

### Introduction

So far we have looked at responses to violence in a number of different programme types. Given the opportunity to edit the programmes, respondents showed a great deal of sophistication in the construction of new versions of reports, or where they agreed with particular scenes, demonstrated a keen appreciation of the points that the scenes were establishing. The audience had not been lulled into acceptance of what they saw by exposure to violence on television. Indeed, the popularity of television as a medium of entertainment, and the consequent frequency of viewing, had not dulled critical faculties, but had led to a high degree of media literacy.

This media literacy, however, is accompanied by a moral framework imposed on a programme when judging the value and acceptability of particular images. What was clear was that television did not have permission, simply because something was factual, to create its own licence of performance.

If we now turn to the coverage of violence by the news, we see the same keen critical eye brought to bear in this area. However, although we previously noticed differences in sensibilities between groups in their reception of violent images, because of various social factors, such as fear of the event happening to them, these considerations fall away to be replaced by a much more intellectual stance concerning what should be seen on our television screens.

The reason for this is that much news of large scale human suffering tends to be the result of deliberate collective human agency, namely the actions that have resulted from political arrangements and political ambitions. Viewers therefore judge the images from within a political/intellectual framework. The stories told by the news are different stories about the world than those told by other factual accounts of violence. The latter tend to focus on the wrongdoings of individuals, not the movement of forces that appear beyond the control of any one individual.

Wars, classic sources of violent images, tend to occur at a distance. It is not 'doorstep' violence and, given that the strictures already documented concerning the acceptability of violent images apply here, we might expect that images from abroad would lack the impact of images closer to home.

The material shown to the groups were examples of war reporting over a period of nearly thirty years. The Vietnam footage had recently been used in a documentary broadcast by BBC2. The other news material viewed was of recent footage from the war in Bosnia. Following this tape, the editing groups, apart that is from the over fifty-five women, were shown footage provided to us by the BBC of pictures of the same event, but which had not been broadcast. These pictures were of a much more graphic nature than those that were actually broadcast.

## *Vietnam*

### *(i) Description of extract*

This material was from a documentary, *The Eye of the Storm*, transmitted on BBC2, about combat cameramen, which used news footage of the Vietnam war. The extract used began with a shot of a plane dropping bombs and was succeeded by a shot of napalm exploding near a pagoda-like building. There then followed a famous sequence of four shots, beginning with smoke clouds arising from a village, continuing with the now iconic image of a burnt naked girl, running away from the village, first towards and then away from camera. The final shot in this section was of a distressed Vietnamese woman running away from the same village, a burnt baby in her arms. This was followed by another famous shot, of the Saigon Chief of Police summarily executing a Vietcong suspect with a pistol at point blank range. The transcript read as follows:

| | |
|---|---|
| 1. B-52 bomber flying low over camera | VO: Night after night |
| 2. Bombs flying through the air, camera pans as napalm explodes near buildings | as the cameramen partied in Saigon |
| 3. WS down road of smoking, burning village, cameraman in shot foreground | their images went halfway round the world |
| 4. Vietnamese girl running along road towards camera | and altered |
| 5. Girl as in 4, running away from camera, now revealed to be naked and badly burnt on her back | the course of the war. Americans could see |
| 6. Distressed Vietnamese woman carrying burnt baby on same road | what had been done in their name the previous day, |
| 7. Saigon police chief shoots suspect by holding pistol to his temple and firing. Body slumps to ground, blood is visible squirting from the wound | brutality without victory, death without glory. Their support for the war drained away. |

*(ii) Initial response and editing*

Although some of the respondents were not yet born when the events happened, some of the 16–24 year old men said they had seen the scenes twenty or thirty times. One said he got the feeling from older people that the horrors of war were shown in Vietnam, but we did not see them any more. He had a sense that the news had become more sanitized over the years and felt that this was regrettable.

The 40–55 year old women did not particularly like the Vietnam sequence but they felt it was necessary to show such pictures, either at the time or subsequently. They expressed a wish that such material either be transmitted after the Watershed or with some kind of warning. The presence of children also upset the 25–34 year old women but they too felt it important to show such pictures. They suggested that such events should perhaps be described on the news and then shown in full graphic detail later when viewers could make a deliberate decision to watch. The 40–55 year old men echoed the need for a warning and expressed a desire for a pre-Watershed version. This group contained two radically dissenting voices. One man would have cut the Vietcong suspect's death from any version, while another man felt children should not be cushioned and should be allowed to see even the most horrendous atrocities.

Unlike their male contemporaries, the 16–24 year old women had not seen the Vietnam footage at all. One woman who had been keen to edit much of the previous material she had been shown, felt it important in this case that the full horrors be shown, admittedly post-Watershed. Two of the group would have edited out the execution of the Vietcong suspect while another would have wished the end of the sequence to have been shot wider. She objected to seeing a man's life ebb away before her eyes.

The 55+ year old men all remembered the Vietnam material. '*I hated it then and I hated it now,*' said one man who nevertheless thought it should be shown for, as another in the group said, it showed '*the futility of war, the horrendous things that men do to each other*'. This rationale was also offered by the satellite viewing males, one of whom felt that the material was the most graphic shown them. Their female equivalents found the material upsetting, but equally did not edit anything out.

*(iii) Further responses*

*(a) Men 16–24 years old:* Throughout the editing sessions the young men had been fairly blasé about the violence they had seen. This was not the case when it came to images of violence in war. After viewing the Vietcong suspect being executed, the group was asked if they would like to make any edits. One young man said, '*No, to me the last twenty seconds of his life are more shocking than the actual act of being shot*'. He was more taken aback not by the actual point at which violence occurred, but by his own thought that he was watching the last twenty seconds of someone's life. The violence was in the situation, not the actual act.

What one viewer considers as an explanation may not be what another viewer takes as an explanation. For example, one young man said that the shooting of the prisoner which he had seen many times before '*makes me feel physically sick because you have just seen someone being murdered, but what was the idea of war, to kill each other isn't it?*'

The picture, despite the fact it made him feel sick, was considered legitimate to show because it had a point to it – it showed what war was like.

Someone else though was more ambivalent about the picture. He considered that the shooting had little to do with the war: it was an incident within the war, rather than what the war was about:

> *It seems a lot of innocent people die in war, but I don't think there's any need to show it. No, there is probably a need to see it because I think you need to be told about it, but that [the shooting] is the side effect of war unfortunately isn't it. But it does make you question why you are there in the first place. I mean is it a side effect of war, or is it a side effect of the political parties in the context of the war. It's like in Bosnia, with the ethnic cleansing that's going on, that's not a side effect of war, that's a product of a political thing.*

This idea that news must capture the essentials of the war – and of course what constitutes the essentials is problematic – was carried over in applying judgement to pictures from Bosnia.

*(b) Women 16–24 years old:* Unlike the young men, no one in the group of young women had previously seen the pictures from Vietnam. They were informed that the shots were taken from a documentary about combat cameramen. One young woman said:

> *There's been so much reporting on Vietnam over the years. We're aware of a lot of the facts so we don't need to see the man shot in detail to know what went on.*

Another woman said:

> *I wouldn't show the man being shot, I've seen the film Apocalypse Now, so I feel I know about it already.*

Someone else disagreed:

> *I think it's important to show things like this, because we only know about the things that happened because of scenes like these. They are horrible but factual and necessary.*

To construct a violent act on film is, given the close focus that so often occurs in modern films, no matter at what speed it is shot, to slow it down. In real life, action is never viewed with such concentrated focus and thus is over, almost, before it happens. The real violent act can almost be missed by the sheer speed of the action (see John Keegan's essay).

The fact, however, that the cinema appears to have captured violence better than actuality filming does mean that fictional violence operates as a base against which to judge factual violence. And here we are on firm empirical ground. Time and again in the course of the editing groups, statements were made to say that they had seen much worse violence in films. At no point, however, did respondents demonstrate any confusion of reality.

If the realistic violence of the cinema has created an understanding of what violence is, one thing is certain: the reality of each medium does not shade into the other so that the viewer considers both equally real. *Apocalypse Now* was not the war in Vietnam. Respondents could, and did, distinguish fiction from non-fiction and the woman who evoked the cinema's vision of Vietnam as a reason for not wishing to see the actuality film clearly knew the difference between the two.

It would be wrong to jump to the simplistic conclusion that the technical advancement in cinematic presentation of violence, and the apparent desire to exploit that craft to the full in contemporary film, has meant that the senses have been dulled, and thus makes the portrayal of real violence, whether reconstructed or actual, more readily acceptable than might otherwise be the case. Respondents did not confuse factual violence with fictional violence. And as we have seen, they were shocked by the thought that the violence they were witnessing, such as in the case of the *World in Action* reconstruction, was violence that had occurred to a real person.

*(c) Women 40–55 years old:* If we now turn to the 40–55 year old women we see the first indication that certain factual violence, although it upsets, is justified by the very fact of its horror. After showing the clips of the napalmed girl and the Vietcong prisoner, one woman commented:

> *Well, I thought that little child, that was horrific, the little one walking away, that was shocking, and that man being hit, knocked to the ground, I thought that was awful, was he shot, I saw him falling.*

She was asked if she thought it was necessary to show such pictures:

> *Well yes I do, because it's going on, they have to show it don't they, things like that. I think you do have to see these things, we don't know the full horror unless we do.*

We asked what time a programme such as the one shown should be screened. The view was:

> *It should definitely go on after nine o'clock. What's the point of showing a programme like that now, I mean Vietnam's all finished.*

Perhaps an important point has been established here about the showing of factual violence. It is obvious that all the groups accepted that news programmes and documentaries should not protect the viewer from witnessing the unpleasant aspects of violence, but because the clips were taken from a documentary about a war that was *'all finished,'* the justification for showing it before nine o'clock lessened. It was not news, therefore the pictures did not have an immediate claim on their attention. These women claimed that the transmitted shots from Bosnia, which they did find disturbing, *'should be on whenever because it's news isn't it?'*

*(d) Women 55+ years old:* After seeing the clips from Vietnam, all the women who were fifty-five or over agreed that the images were acceptable for screening: *'Although it was horrible it was the news, it was factual, it was war'*. When asked if anyone in the group disagreed with the position just expressed, it was forcefully put that *'you expect to see things like that in times of war'*. But when asked, what they considered the point of showing such material, one woman volunteered the answer: *'To let you see the cruelty that goes on'*. We asked what scene they found the most upsetting: *'The lady with the baby was the most upsetting one'*. When asked why that was the most upsetting, the reason given was: *'Probably because it's a baby, as a mother really'*. The older girl, struck with napalm, could also have summoned up the same maternal association, but the cradled baby caught both mother and infant in the same frame,

evoking an image of helplessness. The girl was, as one of the women in the 40–55 year old group mentioned, *'running away, she was escaping'* and was at least capable of looking after herself.

Others in the group, however, did opt for the picture of the little girl burnt by the napalm as the most disturbing image:

> *When you see a little girl running on her own and when you see what happens with the famines in other countries, they are very upsetting. They seem to dwell on showing emaciated bodies, they shock us. Time and again though isn't it.*

Despite her objections to the amount of such images in the news, she still thought it was right that they were shown:

> *Not as much as they are now. But if they didn't show it we wouldn't know it was happening with it being in another part of the world. It's right that it has to be brought to our attention, but things like this seem to be on every night.*

There is a commitment to seeing such pictures, but a set of sensibilities that easily make the pictures disturbing. The crucial finding from this group was that no one regarded the killing of the prisoner as the most disturbing image. This could be accounted for on grounds already provided by the women, that he was not a child, and therefore they did not feel any maternal connection, or that as an adult he did not summon feelings of helplessness that required protection. When the shooting was raised with them, one woman said: *'That's another aspect of war, it happened,'* and then added, *'the shot was over in a split second, he wouldn't have suffered'.*

Perhaps more than anything this statement, *'he wouldn't have suffered,'* provides the insight into the framing of images of factual violence by members of this group. Pictures are viewed in such a way that it is the suffering that is uppermost in deciding the story. We are not saying that this framing is absolute among such viewers, but that to a distinct degree the existence of the frame concentrates the suffering, at the expense of other aspects of the story.

When asked if pictures such as these from Vietnam should only be shown on the late news, rather than early evening news, one woman replied, *'I tend to watch the six o'clock news more than the later news so I would miss it if it was on later'*. This does not demonstrate a fondness for watching factual violence, but it does demonstrate a different attitude. The fact that she did not wish violent scenes to be screened only in late editions of the news because she would miss it, can be taken as a statement that she has a right to watch the news whatever its content and she should not be denied that right. Rights so far as violent drama or reconstructions of violence were concerned were negotiable. They watched, but did not believe that it ought to be shown in the early evening, but everyone ought to have the right to see the news and that meant it should be shown at any time of the day or night.

*(e) Men 55+ years old:* The men of similar age to the women, although taken aback by the pictures of death and injury in Vietnam, offered little sign of the stark emotion manifested by the women. For example, after it had been mentioned by one man that, *'shooting the lad with his hands tied, I can't see why,'* he was asked if he thought it right such a picture ought to have been screened. His reply was distinctly different from that of the women in his age group:

> *It depends which side you are on. If you were on the enemy's side then you'd show it, but if it was one of our soldiers shooting a tied up prisoner like that then you wouldn't show it. Yet they do it, we don't want to believe they do it, but they do.*

Both the picture of the escaping girl and the shooting were considered by this group to show *'the futility of war, that is for sure'*. Nor did they wish to see any more graphic detail: *'What we have seen is bad enough, I don't think I want to see anything worse than that'*. Thus, these men were far from cold about the images, but the ability to discuss the pictures in the manner above, does indicate a different emotional response taking place than that exhibited by the women.

*(f) Male satellite viewers:* The male satellite viewers were not very different from the younger to middle-aged men in their response to violence on the news. Their comments, however, heavily underscored the idea that for factual violence to be acceptable it must make some worthwhile point. In short, it must have a purpose to it and cannot be included just because it is a *'good picture'*.

One of the men in the group after viewing the Vietnam tape and the killing scene said:

> *I think that's more graphic than anything we've seen. That's raised impact. If you see somebody getting their head blown off on camera that is realistic, that's real stuff, it's not reconstruction.*

Although he had seen the picture before it made a big impression on him. Would he therefore have included the shooting in a news bulletin?

> *You've got to show wars, show the public what they are getting into. Yes, because it was a bit of a controversial war wasn't it – whether they should be there or not.*

While the picture of the killing of the Vietcong prisoner broke a new path in British television, this man would not wish such pictures to be extended to the showing of a shooting in a civilian setting. The latter, he thought, would produce fear in the viewer because it was close (doorstep) violence. Fear may be one reason for resistance to such images, but killing, if not necessarily the type involving the prisoner, is an integral part of the activity of war. Death in war has a structured sense to it, violent death in a civilian setting does not.

When asked which scene they found the 'most emotional' one man replied: *'It's got to be the child'*. The rest of the group was asked if they agreed, to which one man with the apparent assent of the rest answered:

> *It's awful to see children suffering when they've no say in it whatsoever. There's a difference with somebody having a say in what they do in a war than having no say whatsoever, which they haven't, that's what you've got to remember with children, they are in a situation they can do nothing about.*

It was mentioned previously that the sight of injured children was a particularly moving image, but the above introduces a new element; namely, the idea of the injured not having a say over the condition they find themselves in.

We asked this group that if they could only retain one scene of the Vietnam war, the running girl or the shooting, which would they leave in and which would they take out of their edited film.

> *If you want impact I think the one blowing the brain out. If you want sensationalism you go for that every time ... if you want to make impact and the [nature] of war I think you show the child.*

A debate ensued about what time such images should be shown on the news. The scene of the running girl was included in an early evening bulletin. The viewer who thought that the shooting of the Vietcong did not relate as strongly to the war as the picture of the running girl thought that shot ought to be screened later. It was violent, but not an essential item about the war in Vietnam, therefore there could be little justification for broadcasting it early in the evening.

When the group was informed that the Saigon Chief of Police was shooting a man suspected of being responsible for the murder earlier the same day of the Chief's wife and children, the man's attitude hardened towards not showing the picture at all.

> *When you find out what's behind the shooting, its completely out of context, it doesn't have a place as part of the war, it's an individual personal answer to ... If your wife had been attacked by an individual, you'd probably do the same type of thing.*

Once he knew the context of the killing, this new knowledge transformed a picture that might have provided an image of war and therefore would be justified in showing, into an individual act of revenge which was not specifically about the war itself. For him, the picture took on the status of a criminal, or civil, act of violence.

*(f) Female satellite viewers:* We have already seen that the satellite women viewers in our sample had a different attitude than their male counterparts towards violence as entertainment. Indeed, their consumption of true crime magazines set them apart in their attitude to violence. They also showed themselves to be somewhat different from most other respondents when it came to real factual violence.

The first comment made by one of this group after showing the footage from Vietnam was:

> *They show that now with a lot of the news. They don't show you them shooting them, but they show you all the dead people laying on the floor, they show you the same picture over and over again and you're not as shocked as you are the first time you see it.*

When we asked her which of the two pictures she found the most disturbing, she replied:

> *There didn't seem to be any reason why he got shot, it wasn't war just there, he wasn't threatening a soldier – she's [girl] lived anyway, she's lived anyway this lass obviously, she's badly damaged, but she's running away, she has survived, and the other one [old woman] with the baby, you associate yourself with that baby – when you've got little kids that's when it hits you.*

As sympathetic as she may have been to the young Vietcong shot in the head, her attitude changed when she was told the background.

> *But if his [police chief] whole family had been killed, if someone walked into my house and shot my kids, and I copped the right person, I would blow his brains out ... his family was killed, so he's gone out in a temper and done what he thought was law, but we're only seeing ... we're not seeing a fair side.*

Her position is not entirely clear on the propriety of showing his death, but what is certain is that once she had learned that he might have killed the police chief's family, she was no longer as disturbed by the picture of the killing as she had previously been.

The women in this group showed tremendous emotion towards suffering, very much in the mode of the over fifty-five year old women. However, unlike them, they could easily switch their compassion into violent passion against anyone whom they thought had committed some act considered wrong, especially if it hurt the meek or weak.

It is not surprising in some ways that they should like fictional violence: they did not see too much wrong with violence provided it was only channelled towards those that deserved it. Although contemporary film violence is often brutal, it still tends to adhere to the old pattern of the good administering punishment on the bad; what has changed is that little separates the good from the bad in the amount of violence they are prepared to use.

## Bosnia

### (i) Description of extract

The final extract shown to the groups was a television news location report from Bosnia transmitted in BBC news bulletins on 17 February 1993. A warning was issued in the studio introduction to the piece. In the item, Jeremy Bowen reported on alleged atrocities discovered by the Serbs after they had taken a village. The item began with general shots of the village, followed by wide shots of men clearly digging up bodies and then by shots of those bodies clearly displayed stretched out on the ground. A Serbian Colonel appeared showing the reporter the horror uncovered. There were cutaway shots of Serbian fighters holding cloths over their faces. The transcript ran as below:

| | |
|---|---|
| 1. Wide shot village, two men walking down road | V.O: The Serbs took a group of journalists today, to Kaminetza, |
| 2. WS village looking down road, soldier on road | a village they captured from the Muslims at the weekend. |
| 3. WS men apparently digging trench | They were showing us evidence, they said, of Muslim war crimes. |
| 4. WS men in trench uncovering indeterminate objects | In the forest workmen were unearthing bodies of Serb soldiers |

| | |
|---|---|
| 5. WS of four bodies laid out on ground above trench | who they said had been tortured then killed four months ago. |
| 6. MS Serbian soldier, pointing and speaking | A Serbian colonel gave this version of events: 'Look at the barbed wire with which they tied them up. (pause) This is where they cut their hands off and then their heads. |
| 7. WS bodies on ground (hands and heads not in shot). Men holding cloths over their faces visible on edge of shot | The bodies were so decomposed it was hard to tell whether they had been tortured as the Serbs alleged. |
| 8. 2-s men with cloths over face | The Serbs had other reasons though for displaying the bodies for journalists. |
| 9. PTC Jeremy Bowen | Bowen: The purpose of all this is to demonstrate why the Serbs don't want to let convoys carrying aid into Cirska and the other Muslin enclaves which they are still besieging. They argue that they are perfectly justified in stopping lorries that are carrying food and medicine for their enemies. |

In addition non-transmitted material from the scene, showing greater detail of the exhumed bodies was available. This was shown to all groups but one (55+ women) who did not wish to see it.

*(ii) Initial responses and editing*

The 16–24 year old male respondents thought the full horrors of Bosnia should be shown. This was not surprising given their comments about Vietnam and what they perceived to be the subsequent sanitization of images from war zones. This feeling that war had been sanitized, particularly in the case of the Gulf, was shared by the 25–34 year old male group. They found Bosnia to be different and more upsetting because civilians were caught up in the conflict. The images shown to them were however, not reckoned to be as shocking as the pictures from the Serbian 'concentration camps' which had emerged the previous summer. Some in the group felt that the untransmitted material might have been acceptable on *Newsnight* or if preceded by a warning. Others thought the story was told adequately in the transmitted version.

The 25–34 year old women found the transmitted version horrific and felt that it was not suitable for early evening audiences. Many of this group had young children and would not want them to see such images. They edited a version for pre-Watershed transmission which removed the voice-over mention of the victims being tied up with barbed wire and all pictures of the exhumed bodies. They agreed that the transmitted version they were shown was suitable for the nine or ten o'clock news

77

and a minority of the group would even have shown the more detailed untransmitted pictures of the bodies on a programme like *Newsnight*. This last judgement was echoed by the majority of the 40–55 year old male group.

The 16–24 year old women were unanimous in rejecting the untransmitted material. Some of the group accepted the report as broadcast, while others would have edited out all the shots of bodies and relied on the cutaways of the distressed men holding cloths over their faces to evoke the horror of the events. Interestingly, this opinion was echoed by the 55+ year old women and men who additionally cut out the Serbian Colonel.

The satellite viewing males thought the Bosnian piece was perfectly done because of the way the BBC *'held back a little'*. One viewer in this group thought that Sky News might have shown more detail. All of them would choose to watched BBC News and all thought the transmitted version suitable for 6 pm showing. They were united in not wishing to use the untransmitted material which they said added nothing to the report.

The satellite viewing female group accepted the material as transmitted. They found the shot of the soldiers holding cloths over their faces because of the putrefaction to be distressing, but they did not edit it out. The untransmitted material was rejected by this group who earlier had shown a particular tolerance to violent material.

*(iii) Further responses*

*(a) Men 16–24 years old:* The transmitted coverage of the exhumed bodies was shown to this group, followed by the untransmitted, and more graphic, pictures of the same scene. No one in the group objected to the transmitted version, one young man even described it as *'benign'*. They took a totally different stance with the untransmitted pictures. They did not think they were appropriate to be shown on television on the grounds that they were not only unnecessary to the story, which they thought had already been covered adequately by the transmitted version, but that they were not relevant to the war. The state of decomposition of the bodies had nothing to do with the war, but everything to do with being under the ground for so long.

Added to this rather crucial finding that pictures ought to inform about the war itself, comments were given to suggest that, even if the state of the decomposed bodies had been valid evidence about the war, the story as told was quite sufficient to complete the picture of what had gone on:

> I think when they said that they couldn't really tell whether they had been tortured because the bodies were so badly decomposed, that was enough, you had a shot in the original report of soldiers holding scarves over their mouths so they wouldn't smell the bodies anyway.

*(b) Women 16–24 years old:* When viewing this news footage, the young women drew a much tighter line on what should be shown. Having watched the transmitted version of the report, one woman said:

> A lot was unnecessary. Just to show the men standing with the handkerchiefs over their noses and telling us about it would have been adequate, we didn't need to see the bodies, our imagination would have been enough.

Someone else said:

> *I didn't find it disturbing, but didn't need to see all them bodies, didn't think it was all that bad – quite mild.*

This respondent considered the story could have been told without the pictures of the actual bodies. Only four in the group agreed to leave the report uncut. These four were then asked, after the whole group was shown the close-up shots of the exhumed bodies, if they should have been included in the news:

> *We don't have to go back and get close-ups, we know what's happened, we've seen them and already been told the graphic detail of what happened to them.*

Clearly there was a difference of opinion in the group as to the point at which the central focus of the story was captured, but the principle would appear to be that there needs to be a minimum of violence not the maximum.

*(c) Women 25–34 years old:* The general finding from the editing groups was that documentaries can show violence in greater detail than the news. It was mentioned in the course of a discussion with the 25–34 old women that film exists of inter-communal violence in the South African townships that is much worse than has ever been broadcast on the news. One example of this material was footage of 'necklacing' where car tyres are placed around an individual's neck and set on fire. When asked if such pictures ought to be shown on the news, one woman summed up the position of the group in general with respect to the different levels of violence permissible on the news and in documentaries when she said, *'I'm not so sure about the news, documentary-wise I think we should'*. Asked why, she replied:

> *Because you are watching the news, people don't have the chance to switch off if they don't want to watch it. If you are looking at a documentary you know what it's going to be about and what you are going to be watching. You have chosen to switch that on, they have told you at the beginning of a documentary if there are going to be any bad parts in it, they can't on the news.*

*(d) Men 25–34 years:* The principle that the news provides basic information while documentaries elaborate on it was echoed in the male age equivalent of the women's group. The transmitted pictures of the Bosnian war were considered by all as acceptable.

> *What we basically saw there were bodies, they could have been dummies for all we were concerned, they didn't actually zoom in on anything that was horrific, it just showed you bodies. You're hearing a description of what's going on down there [the grave].*

These men recognized, however, that each war was different and hence the type of material one might expect to see, indeed demand, would be different. One man, after commenting that the *'Gulf War was perfect for television wasn't it, there was a goody and a baddy – like a football match – it made really watchable telly,'* was asked, 'don't you think Yugoslavia makes watchable telly?' He replied:

> *No, because it's just the way it is, it's sort of dirty, messy little war. The Gulf War was a good war for TV, they could make a lot out of it, but with Serbia there's not a*

> *lot you can do apart from show the convoys, the dead bodies. There's no big battles,*
> *it's all skirmishes.*

There was discussion about whether or not to include the close-up untransmitted scenes of the decomposed bodies. One man thought not:

> *I'd just show the long shot of the bodies. I don't see the point of doing a close-up 'cos*
> *the bodies are there anyway, it's a dead body. That Colonel weren't crying for nowt,*
> *and he [reporter] didn't look too happy, you know what I mean?*

What he meant was that the long shots had established that the voice report was true, and the emotional state of the Serbian Colonel and the sombre features of the reporter all added to the appropriate cues that the scene was unpleasant. But others were not so sure. It had been described as *'a messy war'* and the decomposed bodies, even if not necessary to substantiate the facts of the event, did capture a sense of the particular unpleasantness of this war. This relates to our earlier point of truth as bare fact, either something occurred or it did not occur. If then the purpose of the news was to show that the war was nasty, then the close-up shots of the bodies might be said to convey that purpose in a way that the facts provided by the long shot did not.

But it seemed that the reason for inclusion was to make firm what had been outlined in the transmitted film; namely, that we were looking at dead bodies. The group were given the stills of the bodies, and on-screen editing took place at the same time:

> *There's this one ... too much ... it might be one second, it might be two. I don't know.*
> *Take the second shot that's two seconds, 3, 4, 5 ... quite a long shot – way too long.*
> *You could have that couldn't you.*

The final verdict was that two seconds of the untransmitted footage were to be included in their edit. This met with the approval of those who thought that the report ought to establish more clearly the human status of the deceased. Commenting on the new version, one man with approval, said: *'It makes you sure that they are ... it is actually a body, a proper body'.*

In the end, because decomposition had worked its course, those in favour of showing the bodies became less certain about including what they had just inserted into the film. If it was not a clearly identifiable body that they had managed to assemble in the report, then there was less point in including the new shots than they had originally thought.

What we see in this close editing, and the debate surrounding the value of including certain shots, is that these men were not attempting to increase the impact of the story by the inclusion of violent imagery to make some artistic truth, but to use the pictures to verify what was been claimed by the voice report – that the covered bodies seen in the long shot were indeed bodies. This group used pictures to establish truth as facts.

*(e) Men 40–55 years old:* The men in the next age group, 40–55, took a similar line with regard to the use of pictures to establish truth. In discussing the transmitted version, one man said:

> *They have got to actually show you the evidence because that Serb commander was*

> stood there and he's sort of saying, we've got graves where they've tortured people, they've chopped their hands off. Even if the reporter said yes they took us and they showed us these, I don't think it would have had the same impact that showing us what they've shown us has had.

This viewer had to 'see with his own eyes' what had taken place. He did not want to have to take it on trust. Furthermore, the actual viewing of the dead bodies lent greater 'impact' to the report, by which one presumes he meant that it gave greater authority to the story. However, he did confess that the impact of the dead bodies was mediated by the fact that the death shown was from a distant war: 'It's like happening two thousand miles away so it has no real direct influence on me'. When asked whether the pictures come from some outrage like Enniskillen, the pictures would have disturbed him more, he replied: 'Yes, I'm isolated from that [Bosnia] and really apart from religion, I've no idea what the thing's about'.

It was mentioned much earlier in discussing the reconstruction of violence that 'doorstep', or close news, disturbs more than distant news. Had he understood the nature of the war then possibly his response to the images of violence would have been stronger.

*(f) Women 40–55 years old:* The 40–55 year old women viewed the conflict in Bosnia and the images of the war in terms that could best be described as lessons of universal human suffering. One of the women said how upset she was with what was happening in Bosnia:

> There's some horrific things from Bosnia just now. Some of those poor people, and that couple, an elderly couple, walked out of a place they had nothing on did they. You just don't believe things like that happen. You want to help them, but what can you do? You don't believe how lucky we are, and that's why we should see these things to make us realize.

The idea that we should see things to make us realize 'how lucky we are' is hardly captured in the concept of news as 'a mission to explain,' but nevertheless, if the news from Bosnia did not explain the reason for the suffering, it certainly exposed the suffering. This woman continued by saying:

> I'm certainly hardening to these things that still upset you. You like to see them, but it doesn't alter the fact that it upsets you and you feel emotional about it. I cry my eyes out over all these things. I get so upset.

This group had a high sensitivity to any images of distress. Absent from their comments was any debate about the validity of showing scenes on the grounds that they added nothing to the story. On seeing the transmitted clip:

> I think it's terrible, but I think we've got to know what's going on. You just can't push it aside and ... what's the saying, 'what you don't see you don't worry about'.

What they were particularly concerned by was the description that the men had been mutilated. They were asked, therefore, if they wanted the voice report altered:

> It was more disturbing because you couldn't see that they had dismembered them. To kill them is one thing, but chop their hands and heads off, it was the description.

Because they seemed so shocked by the images, the same question was repeated: did they wish to make any edits?

> *Oh no. You have to let us know what's happened. I think it's important for everybody to know what they're doing, what horrible people.*

It might be expected that this group would balk at showing the pictures of the decomposed bodies, but not so. We showed the film. One woman said, *'They could have put it in, because it was no worse than anything else we've seen'.*

Hence, the pictures of the dead bodies that others did not wish shown on grounds that it added nothing to the story, remained an essential part of the story for them because of the reflection of human misery. The story was about the horror of war.

*(g) Men 40–55 years old:* The men of the same age were not pushing the horror aside by deciding not to include the bodies in their version of the report, but pushing aside facts that did not appear to add any further support for the main thrust of the story. The fact that the women could not, by their own account, distinguish whether the bodies had been decapitated or not, a fact important to the men, was not important in deciding whether to include the scene. It was the image that mattered, not factual detail, since it was the image that fuelled the feeling of horror.

In understanding the reaction to images of violence, especially so in the case of factual violence, it is essential to understand the framework of sensibilities and rationality that viewers bring to the news. Reaction and acceptance have different roots to that operating in the case of fictional violence. In terms of factual violence, they are not so much a question of taste and decency as for fictional violence. Other much more powerful judgements are at work.

*(h) Women 55+ years old:* The over fifty-five women placed similar understandings on the news as had the immediately younger group of women. It was as if their sensitivity to suffering, or concern about the plight of people, gave rise to viewing the news in terms of tragedy rather than events. Their very sensitivity to images of pain produced far more comment in the course of the editing that too much news of suffering was shown on television than was heard from the men – but then they registered more suffering in news items than men.

The pictures we showed of the war in Bosnia brought a different and strange response from these women than from respondents in most other groups.

> *Shocking, can't believe its happening today. At least they didn't show you the severed hands, just told you about them, that would have been sick.*

Although these women were the most easily upset of any of the participants in the editing exercises by the pictures of injury, they did not wish for the news to exercise restraint. It was also the case that they showed a dislike of watching fictional violence, and objected strongly to re-constructed violence that moved in a dramatic direction. It is of special interest, therefore, that they did not wish the news to be toned down if it were considered appropriate to show the gruesome effects of violence, or acts of violence themselves.

*(i) Men 55+ years old:* When asked if they found the pictures from Bosnia disturbing, one man replied:

*Not particularly. It was reality. We have seen it all before. It saddens me. I'm surprised they have let it go on so long this business.*

Asked if it should be transmitted on the early evening news, he agreed it should: *'To be honest, I don't think there is anything dodgey about that'*. What protected the film from being 'too dodgey' was the fact that *'there's no close-ups'*. He continued: *'The description coming over is enough without being too much. It's no worse than you see in Northern Ireland'*.

By comparing the pictures from Bosnia with pictures from Northern Ireland these men were not exhibiting signs that they had become 'dehumanized' by watching violent news. The pictures did not shock only in the sense that they conformed to the expected images made possible by contemporary news gathering techniques, and did not introduce shots that might have jarred by breaking the conventions of coverage. The shot to the head of the Vietcong prisoner did jolt the respondents for the very reason that, not accustomed to the sight of actual killings on the news, it came as a complete surprise. As one of the young men said earlier in describing his reaction, *'it's like, Jesus, he's shot him'*.

Exposure is not a protection for feelings, and the manner in which female respondents discussed the images when compared with the men, showed very clearly that images of death in the two cases operated on a different base of sentiment and a different way of interpreting images of violence.

These men did not wish for the pictures to be inserted into their edited version of the news, not on grounds of gruesomeness, but like many other respondents, because they added nothing intellectually or evidentially to the story, while increasing the sense of horror.

*(j) Male satellite viewers:* The attitude of male satellite viewers towards the pictures from Bosnia was marked by the same careful judgement that they displayed in deliberating over what shots should be shown from Vietnam. Again, the pictures could only be justified if the point that they were intending to make was accepted. They did not, however, find the transmitted pictures very gruesome or upsetting. One man said that he did not find *'anything offensive,'* but commented:

*Initially it was a bit of a propaganda campaign, even though I am not disputing the facts, there was a lot of things done there for the camera.*

This was added to by another person:

*I thought it was perfectly done. You didn't need to see the decapitations. I don't think it left you in any doubt. It got the message across ... you don't actually see them dragging bodies out of the trench. It got an offensive message across without being offensive.*

The group was shown the untransmitted pictures of the bodies:

*I don't think it adds anything to the story, a camera focusing in on a dismembered or decomposed body as it were because he had been buried, that's what they were trying to say.*

*(k) Female satellite viewers:* After watching the broadcast pictures, one of these women

commented, in referring to the devotees of the crime magazines, '*I don't read all those books, and I don't watch those films,*' and then went on to say:

> *You've a right to know what's going on. And it's your choice whether you turn the news on or off. Sometimes you need to know what's going on. I don't understand the politics of any of it, but you still need to know what's going on where.*

> *No not really, it's reality. There was actually nothing there at all was there, and there was no close-ups, they didn't actually show you a headless body, it seemed all right.*

Such a comment is reasonably in line with what many others had said, although to say there was '*nothing there at all*' if true would make the warning by the BBC that 'some people might find some of the scenes disturbing' redundant. The above comment was followed by the observation: '*That's what happened to them, wasn't it?*' She found '*the most distressing part was when you see them standing there with hankies over their mouth*'. She nevertheless claimed that she would keep the scene in, '*because you need to know what happened so you can try and understand it*'.

They were shown the untransmitted version of the exhumed bodies:

> *I think it was best taking that out, the close-ups, you got the message without having to see that, you knew the bodies were there, but when you could actually nearly make a face out, it brought it here, you realized it was somebody's husband, or somebody's father.*

When it was asked, would such pictures be acceptable if they went out 'very late at night,' the answer was:

> *No. It shouldn't be shown, you see stuff like that on horror films, but it's not the same. It wouldn't really change the report to see the heads, you see the bodies and you know what's happened.*

What was interesting about the statements of this group, especially the last two quotations, was that although they did not wish for any more explicit detail than any other group, they quickly moved to include points of violence that others did not. The conversation, and this was true throughout the discussion of all the clips shown, not just those from Bosnia, failed to focus on issues within the clips and moved to include thoughts that enhanced the violence seen. For example, no one in any of the groups considered the bodies in the grave as representing husbands or '*someone's father*'. She said: '*Everybody's body looks like a body, but then it becomes an individual which is more heart-rending*'. It would be. And that is why no one else did it, or perhaps of more relevance, were capable of doing it.

## Editing conclusions

It was very clear, indeed unanimous from the groups, that viewers demand context. Whether a violent event was acceptable, whether it should be shown on television or not, depended on the context, including the time of transmission. Most respondents in the groups understood the concept of the Watershed and found it important, for they thought that children should be protected from certain kinds of programming. They made it clear that there were places in the schedule for factual violent material as long as it was transmitted with good reason. A significant number of the sample said they found the material shown to them shocking, disturbing or upsetting, but said it was necessary to see such things because that's what the world was about.

Despite that, the groups did edit some of the material. When given the facility to produce, they did create their own versions, which sometimes made things clearer but which often made things less distressing. In one particular case they said the editing *'softened it'*. This was an accurate description of all the editing work that respondents did. For example, with the close-up of the man who had his ear bitten off, many groups left the shot in but used it less often and placed it later in the piece when it was less likely to shock. In the same extract, they took words out of the voice-over such as 'tore', 'ripping sensation' and 'spitting out' the ear, but nevertheless wanted the reality of the event still to be portrayed. There were certain instances, however, particularly the Nilsen interview, where respondents simply did not want the material shown.

There were quite subtle distinctions made. The most interesting example was provided by the 40–55 year old women. They wished to change the sequence of the man escaping from the flat in the *World in Action* extract. They moved the voice-over, so that instead of having a loud noise which confused and distressed them, the reassuring explanation of what was happening came at the same time as the potentially ambiguous picture. At a very detailed level, this was a demand for context and explanation in place of an uncertain and upsetting visual event.

The only case of people wanting to put something in that was not already there came from some of the 25–34 year old men who actually thought one aspect of the *Crimewatch* reconstruction, the photograph of the woman's cut face, was not graphic enough. They wished to insert a more detailed colour photo.

The editing method, by compelling respondents to comment on the minute details of audio-visual texts, produces not just reconceived material, but offers an insight into the dynamics of audience perception. Clichés about the primacy of the visual do not hold up to audience response which very often centred on the words used in an individual report. Particularly in news bulletins and in rapidly assembled current affairs material, there is a widespread use of 'wallpaper'. This is footage whose sole purpose is to provide pictures to go over a reporter's voice track. Such voice-overs provide the substance of the story, with the pictures clearly subsidiary. The TVS court case report shown during this research was an example of this – the shots of the wine bar sign, zooming out to reveal the exterior of the building, and the daylight shot of the street where the fight took place. Interestingly, respondents edited out both these unnecessary pictures and individual words and phrases in voice-over to which they objected. The pictures they removed for being irrelevant, but parts of the voice track were excised because they were too detailed.

While in many ways the opposite of hastily acquired news pictures, the highly stylized visuals of the *World in Action* reconstruction were also visual supplements to a story told primarily in words. The predominant viewer response to this material was to remove visuals that were found to be distressing and to rely on the testimony of the victim's neighbour, framed by narration over the more neutral of the dramatic sequences.

In the *Crimewatch* reconstruction, which met with general viewer approval, the key violent event at the heart of the reconstruction was related by the victim in an interview supplemented only by the photograph of her wounds. Full dramatic reconstruction of the actual attack, however portrayed, would have been redundant. Particularly in the case of violent material, it seems viewers needed a minimum of information in order to receive the message. Anything beyond a certain point, they deemed redundant and edited out.

The Vietnam material was as violent a piece as was shown to the groups, but it was rarely edited. It appeared in context, with words and pictures supplementing each other. There was nothing respondents found redundant or gratuitous in the piece. The violence appeared in a documentary of a certain type which clearly signalled itself, and, while transmitted pre-Watershed, groups felt it was a truth that had to shown.

Some material, like the detached, emotionless recounting of his crimes by Dennis Nilsen, respondents felt they did not need to know about at all.

The actual details of on-screen violence are far from the only factors in determining viewer response. The murder of a young boy earlier in the year was reported with immense discretion with no violent details appearing on the screen. This event however, was more upsetting than an actual on-screen execution/murder for a number of reasons. It was closer to home in time and space and, unlike images of Vietnam, appeared to be a random gratuitous event without context.

From all these findings, we believe we can establish certain principles governing the response to the broadcasting of factual violence. There would appear to be four main principles:

### 1. *The principle of closeness*

That viewers find close violence more disturbing than distant violence. That is, violence that they can relate to their own life has a greater power to disturb than other violence.

### 2. *The principle of certainty*

An act of violence to a person will shock less if the viewer understands what is happening in the violent scene -if they know the outcome of what is taking place.

### 3. *The principle of status*

The greater the sympathy the viewer has with persons who suffer violence, the greater will be the disturbance to the viewer. This principle also states that a high degree of violent imagery will be tolerated if the person who has suffered the violence is seen to have a low claim to be regarded justly.

## 4. The principle of minimalism

Images of actual or real violence ought not to go beyond a point of graphic detail once the point which the violence is supposed to illustrate has been established.

The viewers in this study then, offered a complex response to a multi-faceted topic. The editing method added new dimensions and detail to our understanding of how the viewer responds to on-screen violence, but these results, like screen violence itself, need to be set in context.

# 3. Trend Data

O ver the period of time that the Council has been conducting its Annual Reviews, it has asked a series of questions in the quantitative stage that have remained constant so that changes over time, if any, may be monitored. The following section considers this series of questions and notes variations where they have occurred.

## Availability of televisual equipment

### Table 1. Ownership of television sets

| Base | Total sample 100% | Households with children 37% |
|---|---|---|
|  | % | % |
| 1 | 34 | 29 |
| 2 | 37 | 35 |
| 3+ | 29 | 36 |

### Table 2. Ownership of other home entertainment

| Base | Total sample 100% | Households with children 37% |
|---|---|---|
|  | % | % |
| VCR | 85 | 94 |
| Radio | 97 | 96 |
| Cable | 4 | 6 |
| Satellite TV* | 25 | 33 |

*Sample boosted to ensure sufficient numbers for analysis.

In those homes with children, 35 per cent had television sets in the children's bedrooms. Where the child was under 10 years of age this fell to 28 per cent, but rose to 60 per cent of homes where the child was older.

Twenty-four per cent of homes with children had more than one video cassette recorder, and 11 per cent had VCRs in the child's bedroom.

## Viewing habits

Respondents were asked with whom they viewed television in the early evening. Obviously the presence of children affected the results as Table 3 shows. However the television in the child's bedroom would also seem to affect the amount of television viewed together in the early evening.

### Table 3. Watch television in early evening with ...

|  | Total sample | Households with children | Children with TV in bedroom* |
|---|---|---|---|
| Base | 100% | 37% | 35% |
|  | % | % | % |
| Partner | 52 | 52 | 51 |
| Parent | 13 | 17 | 15 |
| Child | 35 | 78 | 74 |
| Alone | 23 | 7 | 10 |

Base: Those watching at this time; percentages may add up to more than 100 per cent.
*Based on households with children.

Interestingly in those homes where children have television sets in their rooms, there would appear to be a greater amount of communal viewing in the late evening than might be expected.

### Table 4. Watch television in late evening with ...

|  | Total sample | Households with children | Children with TV in bedroom* |
|---|---|---|---|
| Base | 100% | 37% | 35% |
|  | % | % | % |
| Partner | 58 | 68 | 67 |
| Parent | 12 | 18 | 15 |
| Child | 10 | 11 | 21 |
| Alone | 29 | 16 | 15 |

Base: Those watching at this time; percentages may add up to more than 100 per cent.
*Based on households with children.

## Concerns about areas within the Council's remit

As in previous years the Annual Review asked respondents to comment on their perceptions of the level of violence, sexual activity and bad language in television broadcasts. As Table 5 shows, two-thirds of the respondents said that there was too much violence on television, while nearly 60 per cent said that there was too much bad language. Two in five respondents felt that there was too much sex portrayed, although over half the sample thought that it was about the right amount. Only a third of the sample thought that the amount of violence shown on television was 'about right', while two in five respondents said this about the levels of bad language heard.

Table 5. Amount of violence, sex and bad language on television

|  | Violence % | Sex % | Bad language % |
|---|---|---|---|
| Too much | 66 | 40 | 57 |
| About right | 32 | 55 | 41 |
| Too little | 2 | 4 | 2 |

### Sexual activity

A detailed analysis of those expressing views about the levels of violence on television has already been given earlier in this Review. The next two sections consider the depiction of sexual activity and bad language in particular.

While more respondents were likely to say that the amount of sexual activity depicted on television was 'about right' in comparison with the other two issues considered, two in five still said that there was 'too much'. Half of the women in the sample said this, and 70 per cent of those respondents who were aged over 55 (in comparison with 40 per cent of the whole sample). Those who thought there was 'too much' violence on television were also more likely to say that there was 'too much' sex depicted (58 per cent of this sample).

Once again, men were more likely to say that there was about the right amount of sex on television (64 per cent of the male sample); respondents aged under 44 were also significantly more likely to agree with this (73 per cent). Satellite viewers (64 per cent) and those with children in the household (69 per cent) tended to agree with this as well. Those who said that there was 'too little' sex on television were small in number and tended to be male, under 24 years of age and C2D.

Table 6. Levels of sex on television

|  | % |
|---|---|
| Too much | 40 |
| About right | 55 |
| Too little | 4 |

### Bad language

Finally, a consideration of bad language on television shows that women and those over 45 years old were more likely to say that there was 'too much' bad language on television in comparison with the sample as a whole (64 per cent and 75 per cent respectively in comparison with 57 per cent). Those who said that there was 'too much' violence on television also thought there was 'too much' bad language.

Men and the younger respondents – those aged under 34 – were more likely to consider the levels 'about right' (47 per cent and 58 per cent respectively). Respondents who also had access to satellite television and those with children at home tended to agree with this statement as well (48 per cent and 52 per cent in comparison with 41 per cent across the sample).

### Table 7. Levels of bad language on television

|  | % |
| --- | --- |
| Too much | 57 |
| About right | 41 |
| Too little | 2 |

In each of these three cases – violence, sexual activity and bad language – gender was a prime discriminator, although age would appear to have been even more important.

The analysis derived from the above set of questions was also able to distinguish the relative order in which each of these issues were placed, as Table 8 shows.

### Table 8. Respondents considering levels of violence, sex and bad language

|  | % |
| --- | --- |
| Those saying all three | 31 |
| 'Too much bad language/violence' only | 16 |
| 'Too much violence' only | 14 |
| 'Too much bad language' only | 6 |
| 'Too much sex/violence' only | 4 |
| 'Too much sex/bad language' only | 2 |
| 'Too much sex' only | 1 |

By far the largest group were those who said there was 'too much' of all three – violence, sex and bad language. These were marginally more likely to be women (39 per cent), either in the 55–64 age bracket (44 per cent) or over 60 (64 per cent). Those who practised a formal religion regularly were significantly more likely to belong here (50 per cent of that group) and those who had taken the most measures for their personal security (more than eleven measures) were also likely (37 per cent) to fall into this category.

More respondents, however, commented specifically on the level of violence on television than on any other single issue. They were more likely to be those aged 18–24 (21 per cent compared with 14 per cent), AB (also 21 per cent) and from households with children (17 per cent). A similar proportion had answered both that there was 'too much' bad language and 'too much' violence on television. This group was slightly more likely to be male and part of households with children (18 per cent in each case in comparison with 16 per cent across the sample).

This is in contrast with earlier findings which showed that younger respondents, men, those from the socio-economic groups AB and those with children in their households were all more likely to say that the levels of violence and bad language were 'about right' when looked at individually. This suggests that, if there *was* an issue that these groups felt strongly about, it was violence on television.

## Changes over time

The Council was able to track the way in which attitudes to these issues have changed over the last three years of the Annual Review. As Graph A on attitudes to violence on television shows, there would not appear to have been any shift over the last three years. Respondents still feel as strongly as ever they did.

### Graph A. Violence

|  | 1991 | 1992 | 1993 |
|---|---|---|---|
|  | % | % | % |
| Too much | 67 | 66 | 66 |
| About right | 31 | 32 | 32 |
| Too little | 2 | 2 | 2 |

See Chart A on page 93.

As with the graph for violence above, attitudes to the levels of sexual activity have not changed over the last three years.

### Graph B. Sex

|  | 1991 | 1992 | 1993 |
|---|---|---|---|
|  | % | % | % |
| Too much | 41 | 41 | 40 |
| About right | 54 | 54 | 55 |
| Too little | 4 | 4 | 4 |

See Chart B on page 93.

There would appear, however, to be a decrease in the number of respondents saying that there was 'too much' bad language on television in recent years, with a commensurate increase in those saying that there was about the right amount (see Graph C). This could be due to the *'washover effect'* noted in research conducted specifically to look at bad language (see *A Matter of Manners*, 1991), which suggested that a level of desensitization to language could occur over time.

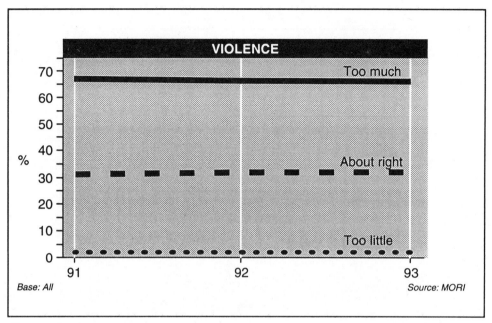

Chart A. Violence
*Question:* And do you think there is too much, too little, or about the right amount of violence on television? (1991–1993)

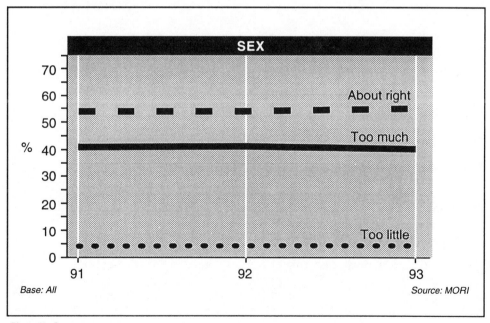

Chart B. Sex
*Question:* Do you think, in general, that there is too much sex on television, or too little, or about the right amount? (1991–1993)

**Graph C. Bad language**

|  | 1991 | 1992 | 1993 |
|---|---|---|---|
|  | % | % | % |
| Too much | 65 | 60 | 57 |
| About right | 34 | 38 | 41 |
| Too little | 1 | 2 | 2 |

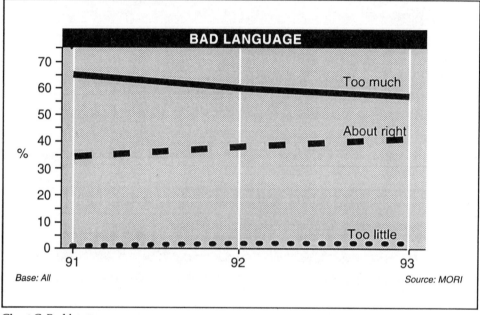

Chart C. Bad language
*Question:* And what about bad language – do you think in general there is too much, too little, or about the right amount? (1991–1993)

*Issue causing most concern*

As in previous years, respondents were also asked which of the three issues caused them most concern – the depiction of violence, sex or bad language on television. As Table 9 shows, violence was cited by over half the sample as causing the most concern.

The second issue of most concern was bad language which was mentioned by nearly one-quarter of the sample. Fifteen per cent of respondents said that none of these issues caused them particular concern. A slightly smaller proportion of respondents mentioned sex as causing them the most concern and this group was characterized particularly by age and gender.

This order has not changed over the years in which the Annual Reviews have been carried out.

### Table 9. Issue causing most concern

|  | % |
|---|---|
| Violence | 56 |
| Bad language | 24 |
| Sex | 12 |
| None of these | 15 |

May add up to more than 100 per cent because of multiple mentions.

In each of these areas, gender would appear to be the most important variable (Table 10) with women more likely to be concerned about each of the issues. However, the difference is more distinct in the case of violence with significantly larger proportions of women citing this as the issue of most concern.

Social class was also important as a discriminator for those saying violence caused most concern, and those taking the greatest number of measures to improve their personal security (11+ measures) also fell into this group (62 per cent in comparison with 56 per cent across the sample).

### Table 10. Issues causing most concern: demographic variables

|  | Violence % | Bad language % | Sex % | None of these % |
|---|---|---|---|---|
| Total | 56 | 24 | 12 | 15 |
| Male | | | | |
| 18–24 | 37 | 14 | 6 | 44 |
| 25–34 | 49 | 23 | 5 | 29 |
| 35–44 | 48 | 29 | 5 | 21 |
| 45–54 | 58 | 27 | 9 | 10 |
| 55–64 | 53 | 32 | 12 | 12 |
| 65+ | 52 | 38 | 10 | 8 |
| ABC1 | 54 | 24 | 8 | 20 |
| C2 | 46 | 28 | 8 | 24 |
| DE | 45 | 26 | 9 | 25 |
| Female | | | | |
| 18–24 | 60 | 18 | 7 | 19 |
| 25–34 | 70 | 17 | 3 | 12 |
| 35–44 | 70 | 23 | 12 | 3 |
| 45–54 | 70 | 27 | 15 | 5 |
| 55–64 | 51 | 30 | 23 | 3 |
| 65+ | 57 | 24 | 34 | 2 |
| ABC1 | 67 | 20 | 18 | 7 |
| C2 | 60 | 28 | 10 | 6 |
| DE | 59 | 20 | 18 | 8 |

May add up to more than 100 per cent because of multiple mentions.

*Watershed issues*

Awareness of the Watershed continued to be high, with 91 per cent of this sample saying that they were aware of it. The majority of the sample (63 per cent) were also aware of the time of the Watershed (9.00 pm) and this increased to 71 per cent in those homes with children. However, one third of respondents were uncertain if the Watershed changed at the weekend, and a further 24 per cent thought that it did. This would appear to be an area which requires greater action to increase public awareness. As has already been discussed in the Review, over two-thirds of respondents thought that there was not a Watershed for the news.

Slightly over half of those respondents with children at home felt that there should be different Watersheds for different ages of child.

Respondents were asked, as in previous years, whether or not they thought that the Watershed would be necessary if broadcasters warned about the content of a programme before its transmission. Of those respondents who had an opinion, 57 per cent thought that a Watershed would still be necessary, echoing indications found elsewhere in this research and in other surveys commissioned by the Council that warnings would be used by the viewer in conjunction with the Watershed.

Respondents were once again asked who should take most responsibility for what children watch before the Watershed – parents or broadcasters. As in previous years, this study has found that the great majority of respondents with children at home said that parents should take the most responsibility, both before and after the Watershed. However, in the period before 9.00 pm it was expected that broadcasters would take more care over what might be presented to children (see Table 11).

Table 11. Responsibility for broadcasts – the parents' view

|  | Broadcaster % | Parent % | Both % |
|---|---|---|---|
| Pre-Watershed | 21 | 71 | 7 |
| Post-Watershed | 8 | 87 | 4 |

Base: Households with children.

## Reasons for offence – watching with children

The Council continues to be interested in the number of respondents who have felt that they must turn the television off or change channels because they were either watching a programme with children which they felt was unsuitable or because they were personally disgusted.

In this survey, most of the respondents (92 per cent) who had children at home said that they had watched television with them recently. Of these, nearly half (46 per cent) said that they felt obliged to turn away from a programme because they felt that it was unsuitable for the children to watch. This is about the same proportion of parents who had felt it necessary to take avoiding action in the 1992 Annual Review. Half of these respondents said that they had had to take this action two or three times in the last six months, a further quarter said that they only had to do this once in the same period.

The main reasons that respondents had turned away were violence, explicit sex and bad language (see Table 12). All other reasons cited accounted for under 10 per cent of mentions each.

### Table 12. Reasons for offence – watching with children

|  | % |
|---|---|
| Violence | 44 |
| Explicit sex | 38 |
| Bad language | 35 |

Percentages may add up to more than 100 per cent.

Table 13 shows the programme categories and the offence caused. As can be seen, films were the category most likely to offend, for each of the reasons mentioned. Dramas and plays also caused offence – these were mentioned by a quarter of respondents. In terms of violence, factual programming, soap operas and dramas and plays were all mentioned, as were films.

### Table 13. Offence caused and programme genre – watching with children

|  | Total % | Violence % | Sex % | Bad language % |
|---|---|---|---|---|
| Films | 54 | 52 | 72 | 63 |
| Dramas/plays | 27 | 28 | 32 | 33 |
| Documentaries | 15 | 15 | 10 | 13 |
| Soap operas | 14 | 15 | 14 | * |
| News | 11 | 15 | * | * |
| Reconstructions | 6 | 10 | * | 11 |
| Comedies | 6 | * | * | 15 |

*Denotes fewer than 5 mentions.
Percentages may add up to more than 100 per cent.

The terrestrial channels were most often mentioned in this context, in particular the two mainstream ones (BBC1 and ITV) but this was to be expected as they have the highest viewing figures. Of the satellite channels mentioned, Sky Movies Plus was cited more often than the other channels.

Over forty per cent of the incidences of offence occurred in the hour immediately preceding the Watershed, from 8.00 pm. Bearing in mind the high awareness of the Watershed at 9.00 pm, it is apparent that respondents were having some difficulty around that time. Fifteen per cent of respondents said that they had turned the television off or over when watching with children between 9.00 pm and 9.30 pm. One in five respondents had turned off in the afternoon, between noon and 6.30 pm.

### Reasons for personal offence on television

Most respondents (71 per cent) had not felt obliged to turn the television off or change channels because they had been personally disgusted by an item or scene on television. Of those who had, age would appear to have been a significant discriminator with 45 per cent of over 55 year olds saying that they had done so. Thirty-four per cent of women said they had turned the television off or over, as had 36 per cent of those respondents who thought that there was too much violence on television.

The main reasons cited for taking avoiding action were explicit sex, bad language and violence (respectively accounting for 29 per cent, 28 per cent and 25 per cent of all mentions). Women and older respondents were far more likely to mention each of these than men or younger respondents. Again, films were mentioned the most (over one quarter of all mentions). BBC1, ITV and Channel Four were all mentioned by about one in five respondents.

### Reasons for personal offence on radio

Nearly all the respondents who listened to the radio (there were 4 per cent who said that they did not) had never been personally disgusted by anything they had heard on the radio. This finding is in keeping with previous years. The few mentions that were made referred to bad language, items on homosexuality and sexual scenes.

### Complaints

Five per cent of respondents had made a formal complaint about broadcasts, primarily on television. The complaints were varied, with the most mentions being afforded to depictions of violence, sex and bad language on BBC or ITV. About half the respondents had sent in a written complaint while the remainder telephoned.

Rather more respondents (41 per cent) said that they had *felt* like complaining about a broadcast, with most of these being about television. Their reasons were more varied but violence was afforded a quarter of all mentions, the portrayal of sexual activity and bad language accounted for 19 per cent of all mentions each. Other reasons given were the number of repeats and poor programme quality, biased reporting and factual inaccuracies.

Over two in five (42 per cent) of the respondents who had felt like complaining said that they had not done so because they did not think it would make any difference. Twenty-eight per cent said that they did not know who to complain to, and one in five said they were too busy.

Most respondents (70 per cent) would appear to have heard of the Broadcasting Complaints Commission. Nearly 60 per cent had heard of the Advertising Standards Authority and the Independent Television Commission while a half had heard of the Broadcasting Standards Council. Just under one-quarter had heard of the Radio Authority, while 13 per cent of respondents said they had heard of none of these.

# ESSAYS

# Depicting Violence on Television

John Simpson

In a recent television programme a photographer, who had been equipped with a small camera and commissioned to make film about the relief efforts in Somalia and Sudan, warned his audience that we were about to witness a very unpleasant sight. *'At first I thought I wouldn't show you this'*, he said. *'Then I thought, "People have really got to see this kind of thing"'*. *'This kind of thing'* turned out to be quite horrendous: The body of a man who had died from hunger out in the bush, close to a medical post. Much, but not all, the flesh had been stripped away by vultures. Thousands of flies buzzed nastily in the empty rib cage. You could almost smell the decay. It was arguably the most unpleasant thing most viewers will ever have seen on their television screens, and yet there are worse sights in almost every place where emergency aid workers operate in Africa. As the photographer realized, it is quite impossible for viewers in the comfort and safety of their homes in Britain to obtain any feel for what is going on if they do not see at least some of it themselves. There were, predictably, calls and letters of complaint. One viewer called it *'not just disgusting, but perverted'*; another said there could be no possible excuse for showing it, even at that late hour. A sizeable proportion of any television audience is likely to feel it is intolerable to have pictures of violence and death thrust upon them; they watch television to be entertained and informed, not to be harrowed.

Many people who work in the area of news and current affairs tend to have more sympathy with the photographer who made the programme rather than with the viewers who were sickened by it. We know very well that succession of thoughts and emotions which he experienced: the initial hesitation and reluctance to show what is happening, followed by the angry surge of resentment that says *'Why shouldn't they see what real life and real death are like, once in a way?'* It seems strange that people who go to the cinema, perhaps with their twelve- or fourteen-year-old children, specifically to watch simulated acts of sadistic violence, or who sit at home and watch television actors in police uniforms punch and kick their way to the conviction of criminals, should have any objection to watching images of the real thing; and yet those of us whose job it is to see these things in real life find ourselves going to ludicrous lengths to avoid wounding the susceptibilities of very much the same people when they watch the news.

I remember with great vividness standing in the middle of a silent, dusty street in the Beirut suburb of Chatila in September 1982. By chance my two colleagues and I had just become the first to discover the atrocity which the world was to know within a matter of hours as the Sabra and Chatila massacre, carried out by the Christian militiamen against the Palestinians who lived there. There were several dozen bodies lying the in street; in some cases the murders had taken place less than an hour before. The scene was appalling. It was very quiet: nothing but the wind blowing down the empty street and the flies gathering around the bodies. The cameraman knelt down beside one of the piles of corpses and began filming. He took immense care over it. In the case of a woman who had been tortured before being bayonetted, he spent ten minutes trying to get a picture of her tied hands without allowing anything more terrible in the shot. The sound-recordist and I were becoming increasingly nervous: we had already been warned that the Christian militiamen were likely to return soon, and would certainly kill us if they saw what we were doing. I hissed at the cameraman to get on with it, so we could finish up and go back to the relative safe side of central Beirut. He was adamant. *'We've had instructions to shoot this kind of thing very carefully,'* he said as he knelt in the dust, *'people get upset'.* It was so ludicrous that both the sound-recordist and I burst out laughing: in order to protect the sensibilities of the viewers at home, we were running the most foolish of risks. In the end we managed to get the pictures and saved our skins, though only just.

None of this is, of course, the viewer's problem. He or she has the right to expect that we will go to whatever lengths are required in order to report properly and fully on what is happening. And yet there is a distinct danger that the process of producing inoffensive television might mean that the reality of what has happened will be, if not actually falsified, then at least tidied up, made palatable. I would not have wanted to show the extent of the injuries that had been inflicted on the victims of the massacre; that would have been intolerable. But the degree and type of injuries was of some relevance. Although the Christian militias at first denied responsibility for the massacre, many of these people had been killed by having crosses cut into their chests and stomachs with bayonets and butcher's knives.

At the time, I made no reference to this. It seemed almost as bad to say that kind of thing in the script as it did to use the pictures of it. As the day wore on, however, it became necessary to support the accusation against the Christian militias with some clearer evidence. I did not, all the same, go further than stating the nature of the injuries as a fact; we did not show what had happened to the bodies in close-up. This inevitably caused some problems for us with supporters of the Christian militias, who quickly heard what we had been reporting and denied involvement. By the end of that day it was clear from other sources that Christians had been responsible for the massacre, and the matter was closed; but it demonstrated the difficulties of not being able to show clear pictorial evidence of what we were alleging.

There are, of course, ways round the problem. Often, as Hitchcock knew, it engages the imagination of the viewer more to hint at something rather than make it obvious. Recently I visited a hospital in Angola where amputations were performed every day on people whose legs or feet had been blown off by anti-personnel mines: perhaps the worst scourge of the war in that country. We had planned at first to film an amputation, but directly we saw the operating theatre we realized this would be impossible. Apart from anything else, the anaesthetic system was faulty and patients often woke up during the operation. There was no way of anaesthetizing them a second time, so the patient would merely be strapped down while the amputation was completed. This happens every day; sometimes several times. It seemed clear to us that however important it might be to demonstrate to our viewers the inadequency of the medical facilities in a hospital like this, and the barbarity of a conflict where ordinary people, mostly women and children, can be the targets of anti-personnel mines, it was simply unthinkable to show an operation. To be honest, I am not certain the cameraman and I could have endured the spectacle ourselves. In the end I recorded a piece to camera in the empty operating theatre, giving some idea of what happened there as a matter of course but letting the viewers imagine for themselves what it must be like. It was less shocking, and therefore perhaps less effective; but there was no practical alternative.

The fact is, news editors are extremely sensitive to the question of violence; sometimes, in my opinion, too sensitive. As it happened, the editor of one news programme cut out even my piece to camera in the operating theatre. The question of which pictures to put in and which to leave out is one of the hardest to resolve, and can take up a good deal of time in the editing-room. Pictures shot by British cameramen are usually easier to deal with: they tend not to feature pools of blood on the ground and close-ups of wounds, and bodies are mostly filmed in mid-shot. The problems tend to arise with cameramen from third world countries, though French and Italian television organizations are far more tolerant that British television of such things. Even the Americans are more inclined to show the aftermath of violence in detail than we are.

So far I have dealt with the after-effects of violence, rather than with violence itself. This is inevitable. It is relatively rare, in my experience, for the camera to be on hand to witness the actual moment of violence: usually they are not switched on, or properly focused, when something occurs. Although several cameramen were present when President Sadat of Egypt was murdered by fundamentalists in Cairo, there are no pictures of his death. Incidents of this kind usually happen too fast and too unexpectedly for a cameraman to be able to capture them as they happen. It is the aftermath, the body on the ground or on the stretcher, which appears on television. Yet what causes offence is as much the way the pictures are shot as the subjects themselves. A close-up of a bullet-wound or a pool of blood is usually unacceptable; yet even a pile of bodies can be shown, if the shot is sufficiently wide. It is the detail, not the fact of death, that people find disturbing. In Angola we filmed a child with wounds on which the flies were settling. To look closely at her turned even my stomach; yet when the child's mother waved the flies away, the shot seemed strong but useable.

So much of this is a matter of the degree of sensitivity. The more violence and death we see on out screens, the greater the danger that we will be desensitized. Yet sensitivities vary from country to country. When I was in Sarajevo in July 1993 a mortar bomb landed in the middle of a group of people queuing for water. More than a dozen were killed. A camera crew from the agency 'pool', whose pictures could be used by everyone, arrived first and saw the immediate results of the massacre. It was instructive to see how the reporters from different countries, and different television traditions, dealt with the pictures. The Italians used almost all of them: the brains, the intestines, the gutter literally running with blood in the rain. The French used the gutter and the bodies. The Americans used the gutter. We used none of these things: just the covered bodies being put into the ambulances, the empty pram, the abandoned shoes. I myself wanted to use the gutter because of its shock value, but my colleagues on the spot were against it and I gave way. They were, I am now convinced, quite right; these things are always a matter of judgement. What is important is to avoid the frame of mind which inclines you to push the barriers back as far as possible. That way desensitization lies.

In daily practice, most of us who work in television news find we use fewer rather than more pictures of violence. In a famous and terrible sequence which ended with the murder of a supposed informer by an angry mob, witnessed by a BBC camer-aman in a black township outside Cape Town, we showed only the first stages of the beating. On the other hand pictures which have been judged acceptable in one context can often be used time and again if the subject crops up again in the news. One example is the amateur video of the beating of Rodney King by Los Angeles policemen, which was shown on at least half-a-dozen different occasions. Another is the sequence shot by NBC in Israel, when a group of Israeli soldiers broke the arm of a young Palestinian stone-thrower. These things were ugly and cruel when they were first seen; but at least they had the effect of shocking public opinion both nationally and internationally and so forcing something to be done. The more the pictures were shown, the less effective they became. Eventually they seemed to me to come dangerously close to the pornography of violence.

Journalists who cover these things see a different world from the one their audience inhabits; especially in a country like Britain, prosperous, comfortable and still, even now, overwhelmingly safe and sheltered. Television viewers no doubt want to be informed about the world, but they do not enjoy being shocked; hence the debate over the question of 'good' and 'bad' news. The existence of seventy-five or more wars in the world and an alarming rise in crime at home mean that a part of television news bulletins is likely to be taken up by pictures of violence. People whose memories stretch back to 1956 and 1968 know that, unaccountably, there seem to be sudden upsurges of violence in the world which can last for several years before levelling off. Those of us who work in the news business have to grit our teeth and ignore the accusations that we are conscious peddlers of doom. Yet people who would never think of blaming the meteorologists for a bad summer convince themselves that the violence they see on their television screens is deliberately played up by the broadcasters to the exclusion of all sorts of good news which is being equally deliberately hidden from them.

When pictures of violence crop up on television, they are there as the result of the decisions of probably no more than five or six people. Each of them works to roughly the same set of guidelines, but each is liable to interpret those guidelines in his or her way. Most no doubt instinctively want to see more coverage, rather than less, of everything we do; that, after all, is what they are paid to do. Yet there are other instincts at work too. Observing violence and brutality at first hand clearly blunts some people's sensitivity, but such people seem to me to be in the minority. The majority of people in a television news team are fully aware that the depiction of violence requires greater thought and care than anything else they do; and although the judgements are no doubt often wrong, and mistakes are more frequent than they should be, at least they are rarely made without consideration. Under the difficult conditions of war or civil unrest, that may well be as much as one can reasonably ask.

# Violence in Non-fictional Television

## John Keegan

I have been asked to write on the depiction of violence in non-fictional television because of my part in a controversy that arose at the end of the Gulf War. What I then said, in an article for *The Spectator*, re-published in slightly shortened form in *The Daily Telegraph*, was that television news broadcasters, those of the BBC in particular, had sensationalized the war by selectivity.

My point was that the audience, entitled to coverage as objective as could be achieved, had instead been deliberately alarmed by a form of treatment which satisfied the subjective desires of the broadcasters to sustain a 'good story'. My own taste, for example, would have been for simple question and answer analysis of the military situation, of the sort I myself attempted to supply during the war in my *Telegraph* columns. Thus I thought that the correct approach to the issue of Iraq's possession of Scud missiles and chemical weapons would have been to ask an expert, *'What are the capabilities of the Scud?'* and *'Can a Scud be equipped with a chemical warhead?'* and *'What effects is such a warhead likely to produce?'*.

Instead, interviewers preferred, it seemed to me, to leap over objective technical analysis to the posing of such questions as *'What will Israel do if a Scud with a chemical warhead lands in central Tel Aviv?'* Iraqi capability, highly doubtful, as any expert would have emphasized if correctly questioned, was thus taken for granted and its lurid implications brought to the forefront of the discussion from the outset. Such an interviewing technique, it seemed to me, was a betrayal of the broadcaster's responsibility, which is to present the viewer with facts first, to move to probabilities next and to raise possibilities, with their attendant anxieties, only after the objective framework had been firmly established.

I was surprised to discover how strongly the viewers agreed with me. My article produced the largest postbag I have ever received, nearly three hundred letters arriving in one week, of which all but two supported my case. As anyone who writes a newspaper column knows, a postbag as large as ten letters indicates that the writer has struck a chord. Three hundred letters indicated that I had caught a national mood. Their content, moreover, was often much more vigorous than that of my article. Ladies writing from respectable addresses in the Wirral in sane handwriting and grammatical English accused men with household names of treachery. Cowardice was another accusation. Journalistic self-indulgence – my own complaint – was deplored by almost everyone.

I do not know how large a postbag the BBC received but my article provoked the producer of *Newsnight* to a lengthy defence of his editorial policy, delivered by courier the afternoon *The Spectator* appeared, David Dimbleby – who had interviewed me during the war – to a reproach that I had been unfair and Jeremy Paxman to a piece of self-justification. *The Spectator*'s judgement on the exchanges was to include my article and Jeremy Paxman's answer in their annual, together with a letter from a reader which ended *'Everyone agrees with Mr Keegan'*.

I am now not quite sure that I agree with myself. I remain convinced that Jeremy Paxman – who, with Robert Harris, is the author of the best history of chemical weapons, *A Higher Form of Killing* – was well aware of their limitations and that he should have tempered his broadcasts accordingly. It was an affectation of ignorance about the realities of the chemical threat in his questioning which I found, and continue to find, displeasing. David Dimbleby, on the other hand, though often unnecessarily portentous, was to some extent the victim of over-exposure. Early in the war he was required to broadcast almost continuously and perhaps lost sight of objectivity for that reason.

It seems, however, that the BBC may have taken the furore provoked by its coverage of the Gulf War to heart and resolved not to allow news broadcasters and commentators in future to make use of a crisis as an opportunity for sensationalism. I certainly note no attempt to sensationalize the Bosnian conflict. That may be, of course, because its horrors defy sensationalization. On the other hand, the struggle between the minorities in Bosnia does threaten to widen the war into the Balkans, with the potential danger of destabilizing the region, setting sovereign states at odds and even bringing on general war. Commentators have treated such danger with sober carefulness over the month the conflict has lasted, in marked contrast to the freedom with which they invoked the spectre of a new Arab-Israeli war, even that of a nuclear release while the Gulf crisis lasted.

I think, therefore, that I detect an improvement in BBC editorial policy. ITN was less sensational throughout the Gulf conflict – as far as presentation of and commentary on news are concerned. What, then, about the material that is actually shown? The content of television news is proverbially the captive of the medium itself. Without pictures there is no news, or none to which air time can be given, and some forms of event provide much 'better' pictures than others. Thus an oil rig disaster on a maritime platform may hold the news for days at a time, simply because the flames make an arresting and accessible image, while a major mining accident underground, which cannot be covered by camera except at the pithead, will disappear from the headlines the next day.

War ought to make for highly televisual footage – and it sometimes does. The on-board cameras of the American unmanned 'smart' missiles which attacked military installations in Baghdad during the Gulf provided images as sensational as any ever filmed on a battlefield. The predisposing condition for that, however, was that the missiles were indeed unmanned. Human cameras could not have taken such pictures and can only very rarely transmit from the point of critical contact between friend and foe, since the exposure that camera operation requires in such circumstances is dangerous to the point of suicidal.

As a result, most 'action' camera work in war is self-censoring. The viewer cannot be shocked because the cameraman cannot capture, except by chance, the sort of image that has the power to shock. He must snatch what he can, often hoping that contingent factors – loss of focus, camera shake, bad sound – will, by indicating actuality, invest quite uninteresting film with authenticity and value. Much of the battlefield film from the Gulf, shot in darkness and depending on light traces from explosions to supply what visual content it has, belongs to that category. I can think of no frontline action footage from that war which would attract censorship in any circumstances, or indeed, from any other war. I could, on the other hand, easily draw up a list of film cameramen who have died in war in the search for cinéverité.

It is therefore not surprising that film makers turn to reconstruction or simulation when confronted by the challenge of representing war in a realistic and comprehensible way. Indeed, almost all early war 'documentary' footage was simulated, usually to be shown without alerting the audience to the deception. A scene – supposedly the first of all action shots – of British wounded being treated under 'treacherous' Boer fire, allegedly on the South African veldt, was shot on Hampstead Heath. Most trench footage from the Great War was reconstructed. Even at the beginning of the Second World War the Germans – who were to become the first masters of military cinéverité – staged an elaborate reconstruction of the capture of the Belgian fortress of Eben Emael in order to bring the event to the newsreels.

Deception in reconstruction or simulation is presumably always to be declared – I cannot think of circumstances in which the contrary is permissible. What, however, should be the standards to be applied to footage admitted to be simulated or reconstructed? Curious philosophical difficulties present themselves. Good taste, and sensitivity to viewers' feelings, might seem the guide; certainly one should not seek to create effects simply to shock, and particularly not when the suffering, maiming or death of identifiable people, whose kin may be in the audience, is the subject. Taste, however, requires a compromise between raw reality and its traducement and, while we may guess at what the traducement of military reality is, how are we to establish the benchmark of its rawness? For reasons touched on above, we do not possess images of authenticity in the first place. We are guessing. We have plenty of footage of shells bursting, of tanks burning, even of tanks or aircraft actually being hit. We do not have footage of men bayonetting each other, killing each other with firearms at short range or engaging in any form of hand-to-hand combat.

This is precisely the sort of footage which film makers may be tempted to simulate – and present with 'SIMULATION' as a warning at the top of the screen – simply because it is both non-existent and yet at the heart of war. I believe the temptation should be resisted in almost every circumstance. Its truthfulness is completely unverifiable. What appears in feature films – in *All Quiet on the Western Front*, say, or John Ford's *The Horse Soldiers*, an outstanding feat of American Civil war reconstruction – offers a no doubt tempting example of what might be achieved. Precisely because it is the work of fiction makers, however, it must be shunned.

How, then, are television news editors and documentary makers to proceed in the future, if the sort of actuality footage they require is unavailable and they are forbidden by a code of practice, self imposed or not, from supplying the want by simulation? They can, of course, resort to stock, since over the century an archive of arresting images has accumulated which usually supplies at least one example of an event in the news. The foundering of a large warship can be illustrated by the extraordinary, close-range shots of the sinking of the Austrian battleship *Szent Istvan* in the Adriatic in 1918 and the effects of sea-skimming missiles by the equally arresting scenes of the burning of HMS Sheffield off the Falklands in 1982. They are to be sympathized with if they feel such stock footage is overused. Even the viewer gets to know it quite well. Nevertheless I cannot suggest what other resort they should have, except in those rare moments when events do bring their own genuine footage from the scene of the action.

There is a paradox. War makes the most immediate of all news. Of its nature its crucial actions conceal themselves from all but those most centrally involved – the soldiers, sailors and aircrew who find themselves at grips with their opposite numbers, whose struggle for survival determines that they do not have time or opportunity to be newsgatherers as well. This simply has to be accepted. I take the liberty of asserting that there will never be a cinéverité or actualité of war – and I think film-makers and editors should rid themselves of the delusion that there can be.

Let them therefore make that plain to viewers and learn to propagate a 'cool' rather than 'hot' approach to the subject. Not only is that morally desirable. It also correlates with realities.

# Violence and Commerce

**Raymond Fitzwalter**

A live experiment was conducted at the Edinburgh Television Festival several years ago examining editors' attitudes towards the depiction of violence in factual programming on television. It followed the Heysel Stadium disaster in Belgium in which many Italian football fans lost their lives following a riot involving Liverpool supporters.

Three television editors, one from the BBC, one from ITN and one from an American news network based in London, were asked to show what they had transmitted, how it had been put together and the reasoning behind the selection of shots and the commentary.

What the viewers saw differed, and it did so by a wide margin.

BBC viewers saw a heavily edited version of events. The editor appeared very restrained and felt that there were many shots that those at home should not see because they were too upsetting. He appeared uncomfortable explaining this to a professional audience.

The American editor was bolder, and may have felt more detached. Certainly his audience was more removed from a football tragedy in Europe. Using similar footage to that available to the BBC, he took the view that there was little if anything which would give offence.

ITN, obviously relating to the same public as the BBC, took an almost identical stance to the Americans, given that there was little in alarming close-up. They were equally bold. This appeared much more acceptable to the professional Edinburgh audience.

Two different versions of events had been available in Britain. But there had been no great upsurge of concern at the stronger ITN version; no upsurge of concern and probably no knowledge of the more restrained BBC version of the news.

There was in fact further intense interest in the subject and fresh programmes, playing and replaying scenes of violence, much of it allied to official interest in identifying the perpetrators, principally from Liverpool. So who had got it about right?

Intriguingly, at this year's Edinburgh Festival, the subject was revisited. In another examination of violence on our screens it was evident that attitudes had shifted over the years and possibly more among programme-makers than among the public.

It was one of those unusual television events in which the public were fulsomely represented and they came across as level-headed, intelligent and discerning. They were concerned but not intimidated by what they saw – and there was plenty that was bloody and brutal.

Programme-makers plainly stated that explicit shots of the bodies of victims of violence in Belfast in the early seventies would not be shown on the news today when similar events took place. Neither would significant scenes from major tragedies such as the Heysel disaster.

Clearly, over perhaps two decades, there have been rising concerns about Britain becoming a more violent society. It can be particularly detected in the concern of parents for their children and amongst the elderly. It is symbolized by the increasing distribution of arms to the police. But these concerns, although there, are not always well-founded.

There has too, but much more recently, been a rising concern about violence on television. In the past it has been an easy scapegoat on which politicians could blame society's ills. But the degree of violence on the screen has been growing but it is curiously a creation, in large measure, of recent political acts.

Encouraging a ferocious fight for ratings; forcing channels to compete directly for finance and taxing their revenue more severely by a franchise auction are all moves engineered in the 1990 Broadcasting Act. It takes little imagination to see how they have encouraged more programmes exploiting sex, violence and crime which producers believe will win ratings and hold on to scarcer revenue.

When you add further pressure from more lightly regulated[1] satellite competition pressing heavily on the terrestrial services by using an unending diet of imported films, it is not surprising that channel controllers should, as they have, break out in public slanging matches asking: *'Who draws the line? – Jack the Ripper'.*

The danger here is that one phenomenon feeds the other. If today's television more readily, and it should also be said sometimes more casually, portrays violence, it may encourage the public to believe that society is much more violent. And that is something they very easily accept with or without evidence. It is also something many members of society are easily intimidated by. But it does need some dissecting.

When, for example, two years ago, The Policy Studies Institute compared the freedom to go out alone of a thousand children in 1991 to the freedom of a thousand

---

1   There are a number of points by which the terrestrial licences lay obligations on, particularly, ITV, which do not apply to BSkyB. Most of these cost ITV substantial sums of money and create unequal competition. This could be seen as unequal regulation and especially so in relation to the volumes of imported American material.

children twenty years before, the results were startling. Children's freedoms had declined dramatically.

For example in 1971 eight in ten children of the ages seven and eight were allowed to go to school on their own. Twenty years later it was only two in ten.

Only a fifth of seven year olds in the survey could go off alone to play; only one in twenty to take a bus alone and almost all junior and most senior children were banned from going out alone after dark – a sharp contrast to twenty years earlier.

Their parents were heavily influenced by two things – the dangers of heavily increased volumes of traffic and the dangers of children being murdered or abducted by strange men.

The first, not a subject of great concern on television, had much legitimacy as the physical presence of vehicles in any high street shows but the second, which is the subject of intense television coverage, was misplaced.

Television has brought fear not merely of violence by strangers to children, but to women and to the elderly, graphically into every home. Yet murders by strangers are extremely rare. Murders of children, for example, have hardly risen in twenty years.

Children are far more likely to be murdered; women far more likely to be battered by a relative or friend in their own home. But parents do not think about statistics when they see dramatic pictures and believe the offence might be repeated. Children are in fact far more at risk walking to school from road traffic, but it is not a significant feature of news or current affairs coverage.

It may well be that some forms of coverage are simply out of proportion. But it is very tempting as a television news editor, when you are under renewed duress for ratings share, to recognize the potential in missing Goldilocks; weeping parents; police fears about serial killers and tension mounting.

Switching to drama it is impossible not to notice the primacy, utter and complete, of the detective in modern television. There are English, Scottish, French, Belgian, American and Chinese detectives, Victorian, opera-loving, Jewish, lady detectives (old and young), detectives who work alone, in duos, even threesomes – and nearly all are in pursuit of violence, usually murders. Towns, cities, even islands, have more violence, more murders than their population could conceivably support. Sometimes it is surprising there is anyone left! But it is only fiction and audiences do almost invariably differentiate.

I digress from factual programmes, but briefly and for the same reason. There are pressures on our television makers causing them to get some things grossly out of proportion.

But it is also important to look at the same puzzle from the other side. And here I return to this year's Edinburgh Festival which seemed to suggest that factual programme-makers were becoming more timid. Increasing restraint, shielding society from the truth of what goes on around it, may not be the answer to everything.

Just as we may shield the elderly person who cannot bear the news from Belfast so we shield the politician, even the terrorist, who ought to know what they face or what they have done, to say nothing of the bulk of ordinary public who ought to be fully in the picture. It left me with a sense of unease.

It is a position where one first has to recognize that you cannot please all the people all the time and, if you try, the moral of the Biblical parable applies. You fall off your donkey. We should, I believe, start with a policy in factual programmes of being as bold and liberal as possible in publishing.

The second step is to temper that policy by applying a code and there are several available to broadcasters, well worked out from accumulated experience. But they should be treated for what they are – good, commonsense guidelines.

The most important thing at this stage and it is inevitably harder in news, is that the editor should have time to stop and think, to consult colleagues and his code – to try above all to lift himself out of the rarefied, overheated world of the television business and put himself in the position of the average family at home.

If this process is followed, few things go wrong. But two graphic experiences of my own bring out interesting new points.

In one programme we conducted interviews with masked members of the Animal Liberation Front – men who espoused and perpetrated violence. They were strongly questioned, not allowed to proselytize and the frailty of their case exposed. But its transmission was banned by the Independent Broadcasting Authority whose logic was less clear than even that of the Animal Liberation Front.

We put the programme to an unusual test by showing it to both a Chief Constable responsible for prosecuting members of the ALF and a judge who sentenced them. Both felt unequivocally that it should be transmitted to put the public on their guard. But the Authority were not convinced. Nor were they won over when it was pointed out that they had previously sanctioned a similar interview at an earlier date with another ALF cell.

The public interest case in exposing the criminal activities of the ALF and, crucially, their inability to justify them, was strong. But it was easy to block when you did not have to give explanations and the Authority could just say 'No'.

Eventually the programme was transmitted more for want of a reason to suppress it. None of the pillars of civilization fell. None of the worries expressed about the interview turned out to be true. It was a strong lesson, one of many, of how easy it would be not to bother to investigate such difficult subjects; to slip into blander coverage or none at all.

Those who argue that programme-makers should be inhibited, should in turn appreciate the opposite side of the coin for there are perhaps more failings associated with an idle, unstriving media providing superficial reports, sometimes failing to report at all. The specific, evidential inquiry can easily be replaced by the bland debate; the debate in turn supplanted by infotainment.

But we did not always get it right. In another programme we examined the case of a man who had died at the hands of the police in controversial circumstances. There were two versions of events. In one, the man was violent and appallingly abusive and had to be vigorously restrained. In the other he was mildly difficult and did not swear.

It was important to show accurately the conflicting detail of both versions. To have excluded or diluted the man's alleged violence and bad language would have been unfair to the police version of events. The programme was transmitted as usual at 8.30 pm without pre-transmission fuss.

But the public reaction was dramatic and instructive. There was little complaint about the depiction of violence; none about the accusations of police brutality or the unhappy circumstances in which a man had met his death. But there was widespread and vociferous complaint about bad language despite a pre-transmission warning and however crucial it was, evidentially, to the case.

It was a salutary lesson and told us that the British public care far more about bad language in their living rooms than about the depiction of violence, particularly when it has a proper purpose. But it taught us that we ought to have tried harder to anticipate other people's concerns. Had we moved the programme to say 9.30 pm the squeals of justified complaint about language might well have evaporated.

In essence British television, providing it takes the opportunity to consult its guiding principles, generally handles the question of violence in factual programmes with considerable care but it may be becoming disturbingly more timid.

But overlaying that in the past two or three years there has been an upsurge of the use of ratings – getting violence across the range of programming associated with a worrying narrowing of that range. That is a disturbing trend and may soon be giving cause for serious public concern.

It is often interesting to look at American television and, as our system has moved much closer to copying their market-led approach, this may be instructive.

It is notable, for example, that last autumn NBC put into prime-time a programme based on videos of people dying; a tape of a pregnant woman leaping to her death from a burning building; a real drowning, a car crash. The biggest rated documentary was Geraldo Rivera on Satanism.

A survey of a short transmission period of a mid-West station revealed three items on devil-worship; four on vice-officers; four unsolved murders; three on sexual diseases and so on – all just before a major ratings survey.

There have been clear signs of British television leaning much the same way. Given the ferocious nature of unbridled commercial pressures when turned loose, it suggests that a strong risk of a drop in standards might overwhelm a history of responsible attempts to get it about right.

# Enjoying Our Indignations

John Wilson

My concern in this piece is to work out whether I should be more concerned about violence in factual programmes. The problem is that for all the indignant stir caused every now and again about all kinds of allegedly dire consequences of television, the public debate does not get us far. We get indignant and enjoy it. We indulge our indignations, so that much comment about the socially wicked effects of television is seriously over-excited. The amount of concern often exceeds the significance of the issue, whatever it is, and criticisms of television tend to have much more vigour than merit.

When a broadcasting story runs and runs, as did reaction to the drama *A Time to Dance*, in that case provoked by sexual romps, in other cases by bad language, or charges of bias from politically partial sources, or scenes of violence, it is fair to ask whether it deserves such attention. The answer, too often, is that it is a disproportionate fuss.

It is disappointing too that the great good done by broadcasting is much overlooked. An asset for humanity is misconstrued as a force for social disturbance.

There is, further, a reluctance to acknowledge that British broadcasting is very restrained, broadly in tune with a sheltered, off-shore, national culture that prefers the truth to be understated, especially when it is grim. No other broadcasting system, as lightly controlled, is likely to be as restrained. And in the British system, violence in factual programmes is even more restrained than in restrained fiction. This is partly because factual television deals mainly in the aftermath of violence rather than in acts of violence. The video camera, professional or amateur, is rarely present as the violence occurs.

The restraint is not the result only of limited opportunity. It is a matter of policy too. When the camera is present at the moment of violence, much British television news editing continues to be restrained. Consider, for example, the killing in the North East of England of a chief planning officer about two years ago. It was in a dispute over a bungalow for which planning permission had not been given. Because the sequence of events had been running for months, and because it was known the planning authority intended to demolish the offending building that day, the scene was attended by reporters, photographers and camera crews as well as by local officials and police. The cameras took pictures of Albert Dryden, owner of the bungalow, drawing a gun from the holster on his leg, pointing it at the chief planning officer and firing. The cameras also took pictures of the victim as he lay dying and dead. These pictures of the victim after he was shot were never shown on television. The BBC denied them to itself and did not make them available to any other television organization.

Restraint in the BBC was more than continued some months later; it was expanded for news reports of the trial of Dryden and for a substantial examination of the entire case prepared by the BBC in Newcastle for screening once the trial was over. We decided that the motion pictures of the fatal shot would not be shown again. Justified, as they were, on the day of the news, later use was to be curbed. Our decision was that in news reports of the trial and in the programme after the trial, Dryden could be shown taking the gun from the holster but that the pictures had to stop, be frozen on the screen, before he fired so that we did not repeat the fatal moment. The actual shot that killed the planning officer would not be shown, even as a still, unless there were very good special reasons. A still of Dryden holding the smoking gun, that is a picture of him immediately after the killing, could be shown, and then, only sparingly. The pictures of the killing were also later forbidden to a programme from another part of the BBC because the point to be made did not justify the intended use.

The motive for this sensitivity was concern for the memory and dignity of the victim, for his relatives, close friends and colleagues. In the same way, television was decently careful when people were being crushed to death in the disaster at the Hillsborough soccer match in Sheffield. It was all in full view of the live outside broadcast television cameras. But the potentially intrusive long lens was used compassionately by camera crews, directors and editors. Long and wide shots of the worst of the crush were shown so that the awfulness of what had happened was evident without exploiting the fatal suffering of individual victims.

It may be that, at times, the camera is too careful. In this context, it is worth noting that pictures taken and used of the disaster at another soccer match, at the Heysel stadium in Belgium, were more explicit that those from Hillsborough, though by no means all the Heysel pictures were used because some were too terrible.

Critics argue that the restraint is worse than unjustified, that it disguises or softens the truth, an insult to adult people who do not want wretched news to be made tolerable. There is no objectively satisfactory answer to that point of view, just as there is no way to make sure that programme editors will never go too far, as they will, from time to time, in the exercise of fallible judgements often being made quickly. I am not much moved by the complaints of those who want less restraint in the editing and more candour in the images shown. The awfulness of Hillsborough was not disguised by the careful pictures, and my understanding of the awfulness of Heysel was not greater because those pictures were more explicit. This is not a criticism of the Heysel pictures, I stress, because I know the care that went into the judgement of what was shown that day. It says only that my perception of disaster does not need very explicit assistance. It emphasizes also that the margins for judgement, in many cases, are not tight. There is significant leeway, allowing different editors to come to different decisions, all within the bounds of acceptability.

Some scenes on television news and other factual programmes deserve criticism, of course they do. For example, pictures of a black man being stabbed repeatedly in full view of the crowd at a soccer match in South Africa were not only explicit, they were, I suspect, used mainly because they existed. They did not add markedly, not at all perhaps, to our understanding of 'black on black' violence.

Radio, too, deserves a bit of criticism. News reports of murders are sometimes too effective in telling how the victim was killed. Raw words in the medium that depends solely on the words can be very disturbing to no good purpose.

These excesses take us to the consideration that the normal test of editorial relevance becomes a test of editorial necessity if the material is likely to be distressing to people generally. When the BBC programme *Rough Justice* earlier this year planned to use pictures taken from an army helicopter of the brutal killing of two soldiers caught up in a funeral procession in Belfast, we had to decide with delicate care, scene by scene, what it was necessary to show to serve the purposes of the programme. Some of these 'hele-tele' pictures had to be shown, as I advised the BBC at high level '*The programme could not convincingly be done without them*'. But the most horrible of the pictures were not shown because they were not necessary in the questioning of the conviction of a man found guilty in connection with the murders.

Programme-makers in Britain who show well considered, real life pictures of violence, usually of human suffering, are in effect saying to their audiences that the purpose of the programme is important and that the pictures are necessary to the purpose.

Such discipline may evaporate. As the camcorder multiplies, there will, by chance, be more pictures of violent events as they happen, some bearing close witness to human suffering, and, as competition grows, editors of news will, almost certainly, yield more often to the dramatic images of violence.

Not that the trend is always to be more explicit. There seemed to me to be more restraint four or five years ago than there was twenty years ago. Why this should have been is difficult to say. Perhaps it had something to do with the dismal early years of violence and anger in Northern Ireland. At the start of the 1970s, when the shock of politically motivated murder and maiming on the streets of Belfast, Derry and other towns was greater than it was to become because we were not so fatalistically used to it, television at times felt bound to be starkly explicit in an attempt to make people in the more comfortable parts of the United Kingdom realize that civilized values in another part of their society were gravely threatened.

Editorial behaviour has changed again, not wildly, but noticeably. My impression is that television news shows more blood and bodies now than four or five years ago. That may be because, out of former Yugoslavia, out of unrestricted South Africa and other readily accessible, suffering parts of the world, there are more bodies and blood to be shown, and partly because a new editorial generation is in charge. Perhaps more influence is being allowed to experienced reporters who see the violence and its results at first hand and who tend to favour less restraint than do editors at base.

Whatever the explanation, it is all – usually – within tolerable parameters. No one, I believe, can justifiably complain that their peace of mind was unreasonably invaded by pictures of bloodsoaked pavement after the mortar attack on a bread queue in Sarajevo. And when nature does violence to unprotected humankind, as in the famines of Africa, and when military man calculates his cruelty to defenceless populations of children, women and men in the pursuit of territorial ambition, the television camera brings us only a limited impression of the reality. However candid the reporter and lens try to be, their work is a shadow of the reality. The bad in the world is worse than the small screen is able to show it to be. Television is a long way from virtual reality.

This is not the result of choices made. It is a failure to communicate fully, even when we are equipped with the brightest technology. It is a fortunate failure because our temperament could not take the full force of the reality of human suffering across the world denouncing us daily in our homes. Some people do not feel a responsibility for the suffering of others in 'faraway places', but many do. They develop an anxious concern when their comfort is confronted by other people's deprivation. The remarkable response in Britain to charitable appeals that follow on the heels of heart-rending television pictures shows that many people take it personally. Their interest is not detached, and whoever they judge to be to blame, they do not absolve themselves.

The concern I feel, then, over violence in non-fictional programmes is about the distress it can inflict on audiences. This is the area of clearest cause and effect because people have only to testify to it honestly. It is not speculative, nor wrapped in dubious assertion.

Victims of violence are a cause for concern because they get a raw deal in our society. 'Our boys', lauded when fighting in The Gulf or The Falklands, are, too often, meanly provided for during the rest of their disabled lives. Victims of crime suffer too. At times, broadcasting adds pain, as when personal experiences are identifiably revisited in traumatic detail in documentaries long after the news is old, against the will of the victim and without much illumination for the rest of us. In this way, sensationalist television behaves badly. The principal failure, however, is in public policy towards victims, and this seems to me to be in spite of, not because of, the media.

It would be a cause for deep concern if good evidence said violence on television caused violence in society. The thesis that it does is not well supported, and it certainly needs much better evidence than we get from hollow attempts by delinquents in courts of law trying to impress the Bench with the excuse that they copied their misdeed from a programme on television. And while violent behaviour by an individual may exceptionally be triggered by violence in a programme, it is likely that, in the absence of the programme, another trigger – a video, a lurid magazine, an explicit newspaper report, an incident in the street – would have activated so volatile a psyche. It is unconvincing to be told that human behaviour has one cause.

I do have a lively concern over the alleged 'copycat' effect on group violence. Years of experience tell me, unscientifically, that reports of violence in the streets, especially graphic reports on radio and television, tend to encourage more violence soon afterwards. One has followed the other too often for there to be no connection. The same effect has been at work when prisoners in a gaol have staged a violent protest with public and media looking on. But, to be convinced there is a connection does not mean that the nature of the connection is clear. The important word in my statement is 'encourage'. It does not mean that news reports 'cause' the subsequent violence. It does not mean that further violence is bound to follow. Other important factors have to be present, as during the urban riots in Britain in the early 1980s, and as during the widespread prison disturbances some years later. After the prison protests, an important Home Office official tried to persuade me that broadcast news reports had greatly protracted the roof-top action. This ignored the fact that at the time the weather was good, that bad weather would have driven the men down, and that readily available food enabled them to keep going. And when the infection of protest spread from one prison to another, it could not have done so without common causes in the prisons regime. The copycat effect is probably less important than is often claimed, and some copycat effect may be a price we cannot avoid.

We may not be able to avoid the fear of violence either. And if we could reduce it, it may not be our duty to do so. While it cannot reasonably be disputed that reports of crime increase the fear of crime and that programmes, along with newspapers, have a responsibility to keep crime in perspective, it cannot be gainsaid either that the main cause of the fear of crime is the existence of crime. Nor is it any consolation to the old woman, savagely beaten by robbers, that young men are much more at risk than the elderly. No one can reliably say that our media encourage more fear than is justified because the level of appropriate fear is nor quantifiable. And we do a disservice if we demote the importance of the fact that in some neighbourhoods of London, for instance, two out of every three people have experienced serious crime.

In this and in lots of other ways to do with the condition of people, the state of our society is a cause for much more concern that the state of our broadcasting. We are better at broadcasting than we are at social management, usually called government.

# Violence in American News

**Richard Wald**

As I sit and write this, ABC News is debating internally whether or not to send Tony Birtley, a fine British journalist, to Somalia where 'peacekeeping troops' are being killed. This morning, with some repugnance, we showed pictures of dead American soldiers being dragged through the streets. They shocked the President, Congress, and everyone else. Mr. Birtley, after extraordinary service in what was Yugoslavia, is today in Cyprus recuperating from severe wounds. He can bicycle, run a little, and, he says, report carefully.

To decide, we will look at the situation there – deeply offensive to Americans – for its safety, for its value as news. Then we will delay. We try to delay. Maybe it will be safer in a while; maybe we will not have to send him. But the story is compelling. Television can bring it to you, can show you its horror, in a way no other medium can. And pictures of violence can be valuable. They illuminate one set of crossroads in history where public interest, political difficulty, frustrated philanthropy and simple fascination intersect. Mr. Birtley wants to go. If we can square it with reasonableness, we will send him.

You will know that by the time this appears.

To a large degree, that is the story of violence and news reporting. The old Greeks had it right: violence is a lightning flash across the landscape. With luck, it is fleeting. There are better lights, like wisdom. But, lacking wisdom and owning cameras, we use the lights we have.

There is a lot of cant about sex and violence. People, we are told, do not like graphic depictions of either. That is why rating systems and censorship abound. That is what societies dislike. But the porn industry thrives and if violence were as offensive to you as you say it is, Arnold Schwarzenegger would be running a sports equipment shop in downtown Funkstadt instead of being the number one attraction on movie screens around the world.

Television is a medium that transmits emotion better than thought and it has an affinity to violence for the same reasons motorists slow down to see the automobile accident and we tell little children stories of witches and goblins.

But violence is not all the same and news organizations do not look at it all the same way. Adjectives mark out the cliched territories: 'Mindless violence ... Horrific violence ... Unexpected violence ... Unimaginable violence' and so on. In news programmes, the sin is numbing repetition of violence. It is a sin at which we excel. In this country, it is an area exploited mainly by local news stations that routinely assault the viewers with the latest shooting, rape, murder or other horror. Disconnected, insisted upon, highlighted, repeated, it frightens ordinary citizens. Their fright steals their freedom.

But in a country like this that has always had a strain of violence, how do you deal with the facts? There is not a truth here; there are several. Repetition numbs perception. Each murder flows into the next. One stain of blood on the sidewalk looks like all the others. We are not shocked any longer at the tragedy that lies before us and so violence does not illuminate.

On the other hand, there ARE shootings every day. What and how should we report on that? One truth is that we live in hope of heaven but in knowledge of hell. Dealing with the knowledge requires some rules: Do not be mindless yourself; Not every act of violence in the city is worth reporting; Find and report the context; Go back to the scene later and see what happened; Remember that the viewer also has sensitivities and should not suddenly be faced with things you do not want to see at dinner time. Essentially, treat the person at home like a knowledgeable friend, not a series of emotional buttons.

For networks, the problems of violence in the news are different. In the hard news programmes we insist on 'good taste' (which varies from person to person) and we have some rules: Do not show the captive on video provided by the captor; do not linger on the bloody act; cut away from the bodies after you have seem them once; a long-shot of carnage is better than a close-up.

With all the rules and the best of intentions, perceptions mysteriously change. One could argue that it was television and the pictures of starving children that brought the world and its armor to Somalia. President Bush, for one, could not ignore it politically. Where it is seen, television is the bane of democracies and the death of dictatorships. Now, the old violence of starvation gone, the new violence of bodies dragged through the streets has replaced it and ignited a different fight in America – get out of Somalia. The passions still run high, but in a different direction.

In Bosnia, horrors we thought we left behind us brought the world's attention to ancient hatreds. It is violent and repugnant and it was riveting. But as it went on, in this country at least, it went from tragedy to dirty shame, from burning injustice to a sad tale. We became numb to a suffering for which we could prescribe no easy fix (as we thought we had in Somalia) and which was uncomfortable to see. Our response to helplessness was collective denial.

Or, consider the perception that Britons live in a country beset with violence and murder. Many yearn for an older, chivalric time. *The Economist* says that in 13th century Britain, historians estimate, 20 murders were committed annually for every

100,000 people, *17 times* today's rate. If the chain mail chafed in 1293 and you killed your neighbour, ten people would know about it because the reach of communication, except for the very few, was local. Rumour was more powerful than the written word. Things changed slowly. A family's place in society might be grand or wretched, but it changed slowly, society changed slowly. It was possible not to know the misery over the hill and not knowing was a form of comfort. But in 1993, we know that our world is unstable, our place in it insecure and the misery over the hill or anywhere else on the globe is brought to everyone quickly, insistently, constantly. When the chain mail chafes, the murder is reported nationally on BBC, ITN, Sky, CNN, and Channel 4 and then locally on each one of the regional services and then again the following morning. We have lost the illusory comfort of not knowing. The technology that has set the world a-spin curves back in television, into each home, to assault us with its spinning. And because television is a visible, ubiquitous symbol of the modern world, its message is blamed.

We begin to see the violence thrust upon us in the news taking on a different tone from time to time. Good violence is the sock-it-to-them feeling when cops get the crook, our gallant soldiers shoot down their terrible troops, the defiant citizen lashes out at the malefactor. Bad violence, don't-show-it-to-me violence, is the terrorist bomb and the mangled children, the criminals knifing the good person, the mindless, random shooting.

Too, it takes on a different aspect from programme to programme. In the evening news bulletin we accept reality: guns go off, planes crash, the innocent die. It is over in a short while. In the prepared documentary, the power of violence can be magnified ten-fold. The manipulation of feeling by music, by writing, by placement within the little drama can be devastating and needs a stronger, more controlling hand. The error of a three minute report is excusable. The excess within an hour's compass is not.

The way an audience remembers violence in news is interesting. Asked in a national survey recently[1] if television news gives too much attention to violent crime, 57 per cent of our population said yes. But, asked in March[2] to 'tell me the one thing that disturbs you most about the news media', with no prompting of subjects, 'Too sensational' topped the list at 28 per cent, followed by 'Biased' at 22 per cent. 'Violence' was at the bottom, tied for last at 1 per cent with 'Poor writing', 'Not patriotic' and 'Don't know'.

And Americans are not the only ones who say two different things. In India, the Babri Mosque was destroyed last December by followers of the Bharatiya Janata party. The BBC, which has 30 million viewers in India, covered the violence. It was followed by rioting in which 1,800 people were killed. The BBC covered that, too, in detail. Many politicians were outraged. The BJP wanted strong action taken because, they argued, there would have been no subsequent rioting if the BBC had not dwelt

---

1   Part of a poll, conducted in the US by the Roper Centre for Public Opinion Research, in August 1993.

2   Part of a poll also conducted by Roper Centre, March 1993.

on the mosque-dismantling. But in January, when the government moved against the BJP, they went to the BBC for coverage.

ABC News forces all its programme producers to justify what they do to a single, senior executive. He is sometimes wrong himself, but the executive and producers educate each other in their fights over what is allowable.

But then we come back to where we started, individual judgements made in the light of the needs of this craft. All of us are caught in a central dilemma: we want to mirror reality and reality is violent. Reality is other things, also, but the violence of life sticks to television no matter what else is shown. Producers and reporters tend to be good people who bathe often and want to be accepted. But they have to tell unpalatable truths from time to time in ways that shock. For instance, a long time ago Britain thought it was immune from the kind of racial hatred and violence that tore up America in the years after World War II. And then came the Notting Hill Riots. A little bit of it on the restricted television of the day caused revulsion and consternation. That occasion, denied and ignored as it was by many, was lightning on the landscape.

There is no abstract entity called television news. It is a craft practised by men and women who work at varying levels of competence. It does not arrive at the doorway for us to show or not as we decide. In the making of it, the decisions made every day are influenced by the society that shaped us and the society we are in process of making. There is no answer to how it SHOULD be handled, only a question about what kind of people we are and would like to be.

# The Idea of Violence

**David E. Morrison**

There is no absence of literature dealing with violence on television. The outpouring is of industrial proportions. But most of the work consists of studies into the effects of portrayed violence on attitudes or behaviour, and the amount or nature of the violent portrayals that occur on television.

The content analysis, or measuring of violent acts on television, does provide a measure of what viewers are responding to when claims are made about the portrayal of violence, but a word of warning is in order. The objectivity of content analysis derives from the fact that a coding schedule is devised by which to record violent acts, and the results thus obtained should be replicated by anyone else, similarly trained in coding skills, who used the same coding schedule. In short, subjective judgement is protected against by the coding schedule.

Such rigour, however, does not protect against the possibility that the coding schedule may fail to capture the meaning of violence. For example, Gerbner (1972) and Gerbner and Gross (1979) identified cartoons as being among the most violent offerings on television. But what does that mean? It has little social meaning independent of how people judge violence. A dead body is not just a dead body.

Van der Voort (1968), in his study of 314 children in Holland aged 9–12, makes the point that the judgement of children in estimating violent programme content differed little from that of adults, and he then makes the telling comment that violence ratings given by children to programmes do differ markedly from the ratings given by content analysis. That is, whereas content analysis shows children's cartoon programmes to be full of violence, children themselves do not judge cartoons to be violent. This finding is also supported by work in Britain. Using Gerbner's content model, Halloran and Croll (1972) recorded that violent incidents per hour were four times more frequent in cartoons than in any other type of programme. But Howitt and Cumberbatch (1974), in their study of viewers' perceptions, noted that cartoons were not viewed as especially violent.

This discrepancy between the results taken from content analysis studies examining the prevalence of violence, and viewers' perceptions, or rather definitions of violence, ought to act as a warning about attempting to gain more from a particular method than the method will sustain.

While it is not possible empirically to make judgements about definitions that viewers might hold about levels of violence from content analysis, coding schedules are not created in isolation from general understandings about, and meanings of, violence. There will be congruity, or at least there ought to be if the coding schedule has been thoughtfully constructed, between the researcher's definitions and the definitions held by the public. However, as the Institute of Communications Studies' work into viewers' perceptions of violence shows, when it comes to viewers' definitions of violence, matters are far from simple. It is not that viewers are being 'difficult' when it comes to answering questions about how they define violence, rather that violence, the meaning that it holds, is difficult to define without reference to specific acts and the context within which a particular act occurs. Thus, the formalism associated with most content analysis has great difficulty in offering expressions of violence applicable to the textured meaning that people apply to it.

Violence, as indeed with almost any act, draws its meaning only from the totality of the situation within which it occurs and from the meanings that people give to the act within the known structure of its occurrence: sex in one situation may be seen as a playful frolic or as betrayal in the case of adultery. Just so with violence. The breaking of a leg to re-set a bone would not be considered by most people as an act of violence, but the breaking of a bone in the course of a fight would be; the deliberate foul on a football pitch which breaks a player's leg might be considered an act of violence, but may not be if the break occurred as a genuine accident in the course of legitimate play. But the question also arises of not just whether an act is considered to be violent, but of deciding the level of violence an act contains; a decision that involves the considered appropriateness of the act.

The meanings that are attached to any violence are socially constructed, and are not given entirely in the act itself. Although death may be an objective fact, the meaning of any violence that leads to death is socially constructed and thus open to different renditions. Thus in understanding how viewers define violence, we must understand how they define the acts that they see: the definitions are created out of the viewers' interpretation of events and the moral judgements they make on their interpretations. Indeed, moral judgement and interpretation of happenings are inseparable.

In the course of our work on understanding attitudes to violence it became very apparent that, in judging something to be violent, viewers brought into the definitional frame ideas of the rightness or justice of the acts they witnessed. In one sense there was no such thing as violence, only images that were considered appropriate to specific settings and to acts themselves. This being the case, it is not surprising that there should be a discrepancy between the content analysis studies showing cartoons to have a high level of violence, and studies showing that children did not rank cartoons as especially violent – the acts of 'violence' seen were considered appropriate to the setting of the action, namely graphic representations of animals in comic settings. Only in the most formalistic sense, therefore, could the cartoons be considered violent; in any 'real' sense the cartoons were not violent. That is, children did not invest the acts with the necessary social meaning to be classed as 'violent'.

Barrie Gunter's (1985) study of the audience adopted an experimental approach to understanding reactions to violence, and shows clearly that the idea of violence is not something that can be taken as given – whether something was defined as violent depended on a whole range of factors. Gunter took episodes from British-made crime-detective shows, American-made shows of the same genre, westerns, science fiction series and cartoon shows. His systematic study covered viewers' perceptions of television violence of the types of characters involved, the types of weapons or instruments of aggression that were used, the physical setting, and the consequences of violent incidents. In effect, Gunter's study examines the way in which aspects of programmes mediate viewers' perceptions of violent television episodes.

The complexities of Gunter's experimental methods cannot be gone into here, but a demonstration of the benefits of such a controlled approach is his ability to make confident statements about how viewers rate various acts of violence, and the situations within which violence draws its power or meaning. For example, he states after a set of exercises, that:

> *In general, shootings and physical violence occurring in contemporary settings such as those found in British and American crime-drama series were perceived in some-what more serious terms than similar forms of violence occurring in Western settings, and in substantially more serious terms than similar incidents depicted in futuristic science fiction or in animated cartoon settings. Put more explicitly, violence in contemporary crime-drama settings were rated as more violent, more realistic, more frightening, more personally disturbing, more likely to disturb people in general, and less suitable for children than violence in settings more distanced from everyday life (1985: 97, 98).*

Gunter quite rightly points to the importance of context in determining viewers' ideas about violence, and it is interesting that he also notes that cartoons were not ranked as high in violence by viewers as other forms of violent programming. Indeed, cartoons are a case where the violence exhibited is seen as appropriate to a specific setting – the graphic comic genre – and are therefore not ranked in any meaningful sense as violent. This framework of judgement , however, is not absent from other settings in which violence occurs on television. Sport is a case in point. When we asked a group of men in Edinburgh if they had seen any violence on television in the week prior to the research, one man replied, *'I watched the boxing the other night'*. Asked whether or not he considered boxing violent, he responded, *'Well, it's a sport'*, to indicate that the very nature of the activity is premised by violence. Nevertheless, he thought boxing on television was less violent than it used to be:

> *It's organized, everything's at hand. The doctors are there and it's stopped before it gets too far. Compared to years ago it's not the same. The olden days when it was in black and white – getting knocked down and getting up, and this happened four or five times a round. The fight on Saturday, they stopped the fight before it got too bad.*

This is a classic case of how events that exist independently of television are judged. Of course, the decision to 'carry' an event is an editorial one, but in the case of boxing, viewers considered that television had become less violent for the simple reason that the sport itself had become less violent due to changes in the sport's own rules, or 'guidelines', on violence. The violence in boxing, for those who enjoy boxing, is entirely acceptable because of the context within which it occurs. But what is interesting is that televised boxing is considered less violent than in the past, and it is highly likely that if past events were now shown they would now be considered violent because they break the rules of how the sport is currently conducted, or rather, if a referee controlled a modern fight by past standards, it would be considered violent. In other words, violent acts are judged in terms of their violence-loading not only by the appropriateness of the act to the situation, but in terms of rules governing violence in a particular setting.

All human behaviour is rule-governed, and it is the rules governing behaviour that are brought into play in defining levels of violence, namely, whether the violence is appropriate to the setting or to the individuals involved in violent acts. For viewers to witness a police dog attacking and biting a man in the process of arrest may be considered shocking if the level of violence used is considered unnecessary to effect the arrest. But what does unnecessary mean?

In our research for the Broadcasting Standards Council (reported on elsewhere in this Review) we showed a film clip of just such an incident without the viewers knowing what the arrested man had done to warrant being arrested. Most viewers, observing the number of policemen at the scene, considered that the dog should have been under greater control and that the violence inflicted on the man was unnecessary/unreasonable. However, when it was put to the viewers that the man may have raped someone, attitudes changed dramatically. Some viewers then considered that it would have been acceptable for the dog to have gone for the man's throat, and also acceptable to show such a scene because, as one woman said, *'it's what he deserved, wasn't it?'*.

What viewers do in defining violence is judge it in terms of its moral-loading. Viewers not only apply a concept of justice to acts that take place, but, in addition, judge the violence in terms of sympathy for those involved. A lack of sympathy with the victim means a lack of emotional caring, which then reduces the impact of the violence, indeed the violence is defined in a downwards rather than an upwards direction. Of course, viewers will not always share the same idea of justice, but the point to press is that what is violent cannot be read directly from the screen, it is only taken as violent in the process of a complex interplay between the acts witnessed and the judgements made about the acts.

It is quite wrong, therefore, to classify all acts on television that include violence as being 'violent' – as we have seen, cartoons are a classic case in point. For example, one man from Leeds in discussing the viewing habits of his small children said, *'if you take Tom and Jerry – if you took away the violence you wouldn't have a cartoon'*. In effect this man was saying that although he recognized that Tom and Jerry was a violent cartoon, he did not consider it to be violent, and therefore, found it entirely suitable for his small children to watch.

Throughout the many group discussions that the Institute of Communications Studies has conducted in the realm of viewers' responses to television, the level of violence on television is nearly always mentioned. Yet viewers have great difficulty recalling incidents of violence that they find truly objectionable when set within the context within which the violence occurs. The impression is gained that what is objected to is a programme mix where too many violent programmes appear, rather in the same way as they might say there are too many game shows, or soap operas. As one Edinburgh man said, *'There's hardly a programme on that there is not some sort of violence'*.

In one sense such a comment is a matter for programming scheduling and not a question of violence, since the violence itself tends, on the whole, to be seen as acceptable. Yet it is worth considering whether or not the amount of violence on television, and one must add, in society, does not create a syndrome of the 'full bucket'; that is, that it is the sheer amount of perceived violence on television that makes viewers sensitive to those programmes which do have a type of violence that viewers consider to be genuinely violent. In other words, rather than the portrayal of violence narcotizing viewers to violence, so that violence of a graphic nature is readily accepted, the reverse occurs.

If this is the case, then 'gentle' violence is dysfunctional in terms of the preparedness of viewers to accept strong dramatic violence. That is, strong violence, which might be acceptable if viewers felt they were not swamped by violence, triggers the feeling that television is simply too violent: the 'bucket' cannot take any more and, whatever the dramatic purity of the drops that are added, results in an overflow of objection.

If the idea of what constitutes violence is not fixed, viewers do have a fairly fixed idea that television is violent. However, as has been argued, the idea of television being violent is a comment on a style of content, and should not be taken as representing viewers' definitions of violence. The idea of what is or is not violent is a subjective response to objective material that brings into play not simply viewers' attitudes to various forms of behaviour in general, but judgements of the appropriateness of acts in the context of their occurrence.

## References

Gerbner, G. (1972): 'Violence in Television Drama: Trends and Symbolic Functions', in G.A. Comstock and E.A. Rubinstein (eds) *Television and Social Behaviour*. Vol 1, *Media Content and Control*. Washington, D.C. U.S. Government Printing Office. pp. 28–187.

Gerbner, G. and Gross, L. (1976): 'Living with Television: The Violence Profile'. *Journal of Communications*, Vol. 26 pp. 173–199.

Gunter, B. (1985): *Dimensions of TV Violence*. Aldershot: Gower.

Halloran, J.D. and Croll, P. (1972): 'Television Programmes in Great Britain', in G.A. Comstock and E.A. Rubinstein (eds), *Television and Social Behaviour*, Vol. 1. *Content and Control*. Washington D.C. U.S. Printing Office. pp. 415–492.

Howitt, D. and Cumberbatch, G. (1975) *Mass Media Violence and Society*. New York: Halstead.

Van der Voort, T.H.A. (1986) *Television Violence: A Child's Eye View*. Amsterdam, Holland: Elsevier Science Publishers.

# APPENDICES

# 1. Technical Details – Quantitative Survey

MORI interviewed a representative sample of 1296 adults aged 16 and over in 52 constituency sampling points in Great Britain from 4–22 September 1993.

## Sample design

A two-stage sample design was used; a random sample of sampling points followed by a quota sample of respondents within these sampling points.

### 1. Constituencies

There are 650 parliamentary constituencies in Great Britain. Two of these (Western Isles and Orkney & Shetland) were excluded from the sampling frame as being too remote to cover. The remaining 648 parliamentary constituencies in Great Britain were classified into Registrar General's ten new Standard Regions. Within each Standard Region, Constituencies were classified into four types:-

(a) Metropolitan county

(b) Other 100 per cent urban

(c) Mixed urban/rural

(d) Rural

Within these four cells, constituencies were listed according to the percentage level of heads of household who were classified as professional or managerial, according to the 1981 census data. A systematic sample of 52 constituencies was selected, with probability of selection proportional to the size of electorate in each constituency.

## 2. Respondents

Within each sampling point, twenty-five respondents were interviewed, split into three sub-samples:

> (a)  Main sample
>
> (b)  Video owners
>
> (c)  Satellite receivers (booster sample)

### (i) Main sample

Fifteen respondents were selected by means of a 40-cell interlocking quota. The quotas used were:

> Sex:  (Male, Female)
>
> Class:  (AB/C1/C2/DE)
>
> Age:  (16–24/25–34/35–44/45–54/55+)

### (ii) Video owners

An additional five respondents were selected by means of a 11-cell non-interlocking quota. The quotas used were:

> Sex:  (Male, Female)
>
> Class:  (AB/C1/C2/DE)
>
> Age:  (16–24/25–34/35–44/45–54/55+)

These respondents only qualified if they had a working video recorder at home.

### (iii) Satellite receivers

An additional five respondents were selected by means of an 11-cell non-interlocking quota. The quotas used again were:

> Sex:  (Male, Female)
>
> Class:  (AB/C1/C2/DE)
>
> Age:  (16–24/25–34/35–44/45–54/55+)

These respondents only qualified if they received TV channels via a satellite dish at home.

## Weighting

| Cell | Unweighted total | Weighting factor |
|---|---|---|
| *Male:* | | |
| Total | 621 | 0.993 |
| 16–24 | 103 | 1.271 |
| 25–34 | 123 | 0.906 |
| 35–44 | 101 | 0.975 |
| 45–54 | 109 | 0.844 |
| 55–59 | 44 | 1.090 |
| 60–64 | 36 | 1.080 |
| 65–69 | 40 | 0.940 |
| 70+ | 65 | 0.917 |
| *Female:* | | |
| Total | 675 | 1.006 |
| 16–24 | 94 | 1.337 |
| 25–34 | 152 | 0.767 |
| 35–44 | 137 | 0.709 |
| 45–54 | 96 | 0.972 |
| 55–59 | 42 | 1.234 |
| 60–64 | 47 | 0.937 |
| 65–69 | 39 | 1.196 |
| 70+ | 68 | 1.525 |
| *Social class:* | | |
| A | 20 | 1.881 |
| B | 194 | 1.015 |
| C1 | 317 | 0.924 |
| C2 | 367 | 0.992 |
| D | 225 | 1.008 |
| E | 173 | 1.027 |
| *Region:* | | |
| Scotland | 126 | 0.936 |
| North East | 75 | 0.950 |
| North West | 184 | 0.789 |
| Yorkshire & Humberside | 101 | 1.155 |
| East Midlands | 87 | 1.073 |
| West Midlands | 124 | 0.993 |
| Wales | 82 | 0.806 |
| East Anglia | 75 | 1.435 |
| South West | 55 | 0.848 |
| London | 157 | 1.015 |
| South East (excl London) | 230 | 1.082 |

The data were adjusted to the population using target 'rim' weights for social class, standard region and age within sex. The weights shown in the tables are the average weight applied to each cell.

## Interviews

All interviews were conducted in the home, with only one interview per household. Interviewers were instructed to leave at least five doors between each call. Half the interviews conducted by each interviewer were carried out in the evening or at the weekend. Fieldwork was carried out by MORI Field & Tab.

## Questionnaire

The questionnaire was piloted in two stages. The first stage was a dynamic pilot at a central location in Cambridge. The procedure was as follows. Six interviews were conducted, each observed by a researcher from the Broadcasting Standards Council or MORI. On the basis of these interviews the questionnaire was modified, and a second set of six interviews was conducted. After further modification three more interviews were conducted and a draft questionnaire was prepared for the second, extensive stage of piloting. At the second stage the questionnaire was piloted in-home with twelve members of the general public, selected with particular emphasis on the elderly and 'DE' social classes, to ensure that no difficulties in question wording or comprehension would be encountered during the survey.

The first part of the questionnaire was split into two versions and administered to matched subsamples.

# 2. Technical Details – Editing Groups

**The editing method**

The editing work was based on a method evolved as part of a previous research project funded by the Economic and Social Research Council, which used material from the television coverage of the Gulf War. (In the Gulf War exercise respondents were shown three versions of the same event as reported by different television news services, as well as untransmitted material from a television news agency. They were then asked to edit together their own preferred version of the event. This major editing task, produced a new report of over three minutes in length, for which respondents were given a substantial amount of time. The editing exercise was preceded by general discussion, but was itself a specific assigned task of some duration.)

In this new work, the viewer editing technique was integrated into the structure of orthodox focus groups. The groups began with a general introductory discussion explaining the method to them and discussing the general issue of violence. They were then shown specific material and given the option, at the end of each viewing, to re-edit the material as they would like to see it. They could cut material out or indeed say what they would like to put in. The method was facilitated by providing viewers with still photographs and transcripts. Viewers could read the transcripts, look at the still photographs and make observations. They could also have the videotape re-played to them.

In some cases there was not a finely detailed editing issue as such for viewers either approved of the material or simply did not wish to see it at all. In other cases they altered the material subtly. The editing was most often done interactively with respondents commenting on the process as the videotape editor carried out their instructions on the editing equipment in the room. In other cases the editing had to be done while discussion progressed and the product shown to the groups when completed. The exact method employed depended on the complexity of the editing task that the group had requested.

## The structure of the groups

All groups were recruited by the professional recruitment agency QRS. Ten groups were recruited from the social grade C1/C2, split for age and sex. These groups of consisted of 7-8 respondents each and were conducted between 18 March and 1 April 1993:

| | | |
|---|---|---|
| Thursday | 18 March | 16–24 year old men |
| Monday | 22 March | 40–55 year old women |
| Tuesday | 23 March | 25–34 year old men |
| Wednesday | 24 March | 25–34 year old women |
| Thursday | 25 March | 40–55 year old men |
| Monday | 29 March | 16–24 year old women |
| Tuesday | 30 March | 55+ year old men |
| Tuesday | 30 March | under 50 year old satellite viewers, men |
| Wednesday | 31 March | under 50 year old satellite viewers, women |
| Thursday | 1 April | 55+ year old women |

## Glossary of Terms Used in Section 2

| | |
|---|---|
| B/w still | Black and white still photograph |
| VO | Voice-over |
| CU | Close-up shot |
| WS | Wide shot |
| PTC | Piece (said) to camera |
| Int. | Interview |

# 3. Definition of Socio-economic Groups

| Social grade | Social status | Chief income earner occupation |
|---|---|---|
| A | Upper middle class | Higher managerial/administration/professional |
| B | Middle class | Intermediate managerial/administration/professional |
| C1 | Lower middle class | Supervisory/clerical/junior managerial/administration/professional |
| C2 | Skilled working class | Skilled manual workers |
| D | Working class | Semi- and unskilled workers |
| E | Lowest level of subsistence | State pensioner or widows (no other earners)/casual or lowest grade workers |

# 4. Biographies of Researchers

**Brian Gosschalk**

A graduate of Oxford University, Brian Gosschalk worked in the Special Current Affairs Unit of the BBC and with Dr. David Butler at Nuffield College prior to joining MORI in 1979. He is the Director with overall responsibility for Social Research, which accounts for over 40 per cent of MORI's turnover. He is Chairman of the Social Research Association (SRA) and a Council Member of the World Association for Public Opinion Research (WAPOR).

**Brent MacGregor**

Brent MacGregor is a former BBC Television producer with experience in Arts and Current Affairs broadcasting. He has also worked for independent producers on programmes for Channel Four. He holds a Doctorate in Critical Theory from Oxford University.

**Beate Mellmann**

Beate Mellmann is a Graduate in Economics (International Relations) from the London School of Economics. She joined MORI in 1991 after spending five years in Germany where she gained valuable experience at managing international research projects. She currently works on a wide range of communication and media surveys.

**Andrea Millwood Hargrave**

Andrea Millwood Hargrave joined the Broadcasting Standards Council as Research Director in February 1991. Previously Director of Planning (Marketing) for British Satellite Broadcasting, she was PREM1ERE's Director of Sales and Marketing and Head of Research for Thorn EMI Cable Programmes and Grampian Television. She graduated from the University of Durham with a Degree in Psychology.

**David Morrison**

David Morrison is currently Research Director at the Institute of Communication

Studies at the University of Leeds. He gained his first Degree in Sociology from the University of Hull and his Doctorate in Mass Communication Research from the University of Leicester. He was Research fellow at the University of Leicester and the City University. He is the author of seven books on the media.

## Andrew Thorpe

Andrew Thorpe is the Chief Technician at Leeds University, who was responsible for editing the videos in the editing groups.

## Nick Winkfield

Nick Winkfield is the MORI partner responsible for media research. A graduate of Cambridge University, he has been involved in media and communication research in Britain and throughout Europe for nearly 20 years, before which he worked in advertising and management consultancy. He is responsible for the development of Socioconsult, the MORI Group company which measures and interprets socio-cultural trends and tendencies in Britain.

# 5: Authors' Biographies

**Raymond Alan Fitzwalter** joined Granada in September 1970 as a Researcher from the Bradford Telegraph and Argus. He joined *World in Action*'s investigation bureau and became a Producer in 1975. During this time he conducted a number of investigations including *Sailors' Jail, The Rise and Fall of John Poulson, The Squeeze, Business in Gozo* and *The Dundee Dossier*. In 1976 he became Series Editor and, in 1986, Executive Producer.

*World in Action* has won many awards during his time in charge including four Royal Television Society Awards, three Freedom of Information Awards and, in 1987, the British Academy of Film and Television Arts: Best Factual Series. In 1987 he became Commissioning Executive for News and Current Affairs and in 1989 Head of Current Affairs.

In March 1991 he was given the Desmond David Award by the British Academy of Film and Television Arts for: 'An outstanding creative contribution to television'. In July 1993 he was elected a fellow of the Royal Television Society in recognition of: 'An outstanding contribution to the furtherance of television'.

**John Keegan** was Senior Lecturer in Military History at the Royal Military Academy Sandhurst from 1960–86; since 1986 he has been Defence Editor of *The Daily Telegraph*. He is the author of sixteen books, of which the best known are *The Face of Battle* (1976), *Six Armies in Normandy* (1982), *The Mask of Command* (1987), *The Price of Admiralty* (1988), *The Second World War* (1989) and *The History of Warfare* (1993).

He was a visiting professor in 1984 at Princeton University and Lees-Knowles Lecturer at Cambridge, 1986–87. He is a Fellow of the Royal Historial Society and a Fellow of the Royal Society of Literature.

**David E Morrison** is currently Research Director at the Institute of Communication studies at the University of Leeds. He gained his first Degree in Sociology from the University of Hull and his Doctorate in Mass Communication Research from the University of Leicester. He was Research fellow at the University of Leicester and the City University. He is the author of seven books on the media.

**John Simpson** is BBC Foreign Affairs Editor and contributing editor of *The Spectator*. He joined the BBC in 1966 working as sub-editor, Radio News, 1966–70; reporter,

Radio News, 1970–72; foreign correspondent based in Dublin (1972–75), Brussels (1975–77), and in Johannesburg (1977–78). He became diplomatic correspondent, Television News, in 1978; political editor in 1980 and was a presenter on *The Nine O'Clock News* (1981–82). John was diplomatic editor between 1982 and 1988, when he became foreign affairs editor.

John has published a number of books based on his experiences and his awards include the James Cameron Award, 1990; Royal Television Society Journalist of the Year, 1991; Richard Dimbleby Award, British Academy of Film and Television Arts, 1992; Columnist of the Year, 1992, Magazine Publishing Awards.

He was appointed CBE in Gulf War Honours, 1991 and was made a Fellow of the Royal Geographical Society, 1990.

**Richard Wald** was named Senior Vice President for Editorial Quality for ABC News in January, 1993. He is responsible, among other matters, for the journalistic integrity and editorial standards of ABC News and also represents ABC News in its relationship with news entities and organizations worldwide.

Richard has been a Senior Vice President for ABC News since he joined the network in 1978. He came to ABC News from the Times-Mirror Company in Los Angeles, where he had been Assistant to the Chairman of the Board. He spent nine years with NBC News in various executive positions, and from 1973 until 1977 served as President of NBC News. Before that, he had been Executive Vice President of Whitney Communications, Inc.

Between 1951 and 1966, he was a correspondent for the *New York Herald Tribune* and successively held the positions of religion editor, political reporter, foreign correspondent (in London and Bonn), associate editor and managing editor.

Richard serves as Chairman of the Board of the *Columbia Spectator*, the Columbia undergraduate daily, and is Chairman of the Executive Committee of Worldwide Television News. In 1992, he was appointed to the Knight Foundation's journalism advisory committee.

**John Wilson** writes on media issues and helps train programme makers. He was Controller, Editorial Policy at the BBC, with responsibilities for editorial standards in all factual programmes, from 1987 to March 1993, and before that, Editor, News and Current Affairs, BBC Radio, and Editor, BBC Radio News. His working life, after graduating from Durham University, has been entirely in journalism, for newspapers, radio and television, and included two years as a reporter in Central Africa.

# 6. Publications of the Broadcasting Standards Council

*A Code of Practice* November 1989
This publication is available free of charge from the BSC
A revised version will be published in 1994.

*Broadcasting Standards Council Annual Report 1988-89* and *Code of Practice Broadcasting Standards Council Annual Report 1989–90, 1990–91, 1991–92* and *1992–93.*  Available from the BSC £4.00 each

## BSC Monograph Series

*A Measure of Uncertainty – The Effects of the Mass Media*
by Dr Cumberbatch and Dr Howitt
Co-publishers John Libbey & Co Ltd, 1989, £18.00

*Survivors and the Media*
by Ann Shearer
Co-publishers John Libbey & Co Ltd, 1991, £10.00

*A Matter of Manners? – The Limits of Broadcasting Language*
edited by Andrea Millwood Hargrave
Co-publishers John Libbey & Co Ltd, 1991, £12.50

## BSC Annual Research Review

Public Opinion and Broadcasting Standards – 1
*Violence in Television Fiction*
by Dr David Docherty
Co-publishers John Libbey & Co Ltd, 1990, £10.00

Public Opinion and Broadcasting Standards – 2
*Taste and Decency in Broadcasting*
by Andrea Millwood Hargrave
Co-publishers John Libbey & Co Ltd, 1991, £10.00

Public Opinion and Broadcasting Standards – 3
*Sex and Sexuality in Broadcasting*
by Andrea Millwood Hargrave
Co-publishers John Libbey and Co Ltd, 1992, £12.50

Public Opinion and Broadcasting Standards – 4
*Violence in Factual Television*
by Andrea Millwood Hargrave
Co-publishers John Libbey and Co Ltd, 1993, £12.50

## Books

*Television and the Public Interest – Vulnerable Values in West European Broadcasting*
Edited by Professor Jay G Blumler
Published by Sage 1991 £30.00 (Cloth) £11.95 (paper)

*Women Viewing Violence: How Women Interpret Violence on Television*
Film and Media Research Institute and Institute for the Study of Violence, University of Stirling.
Authors: Professor Philip Schlesinger, Professor Rebecca Dobash, Dr Russell Dobash, Kay Weaver
Published by the BFI 1992 £26.00 (hardback) £10.65 (paperback)

## BSC Research Working Papers

I. *Children, Television and Morality, I*
Dr Anne Sheppard, University of Leeds; 1990

II. *Television and Fantasy: An Exploratory Study*
The Communications Research Group, Aston University; 1990

III. *Morality, Television and the Pre-adolescent*
Research International, Young Minds; 1990

IV. *Television Advertising and Sex Role Stereotyping*
The Communications Research Group, Aston University; 1990

V. *Children, Television and Morality, II*
Dr Anne Sheppard, University of Leeds; 1992

VI. *Television and Young People*
John Caughie, John Logie Baird Centre, University of Glasgow; 1992

VII. *The Portrayal of Ethnic Minorities on Television*
by A Millwood Hargrave, K Aisbett, M Gillespie, BSC; 1992

VIII. *The Future of Children's Television in Britain*
An Enquiry for the BSC by Professor Jay G Blumler, BSC; 1992

Working Papers are available from the BSC, £5.00 per copy. Please send payment with order.

## BSC Monitoring Reports

*Monitoring Report I*: 1992 (May 1993)

Monitoring Reports are available from the BSC, £5.00 per copy. Please send payment with order.

## Leaflets

*Making Complaints*
*Broadcasting Standards Council and its Activities*
*Broadcasting and Bad Language*

Leaflets available free of charge from the BSC

## Future Publications

*Understanding Broadcasting – Media Education Across Europe*
Editors: David French, Michael Richards. To be published by Routledge.

*Monitoring Report II*: 1993

*Research Working Paper: The Portrayal of Women in the Media*

## Publishers

John Libbey & Company Ltd
13 Smith's Yard
Summerley Street
London SW18 4HR

Sage Publications Ltd
6 Bonhill Street
London EC2A 4PU

British Film Institute
21 Stephen Street
London W1P 1PL

Routledge
11 New Fetter Lane
London EC4 4EE

# 7. The Broadcasting Standards Council remit

The Broadcasting Standards Council's remit is concerned with the portrayal of violence, sexual conduct and matters of taste and decency (such as bad language or the treatment of disasters) in television and radio programmes or broadcast advertisements. The BSC is a statutory body under the Broadcasting Act, 1990.

The Council has five main tasks:

1. To draw up and from time to time review a Code of Practice.

2. To monitor programmes and to make reports on the areas within the Council's remit.

3. To commission research into such matters as the nature and effects on attitudes and behaviour of the portrayal of violence and of sex in programmes and advertisements, and standards of taste and decency.

4. To consider and make findings on complaints.

5. To represent the UK on international bodies concerned with setting standards for television programmes.

**Broadcasting Standards Council**
5–8 The Sanctuary
London SW1P 3JS

Tel: 071-233 0544
Fax: 071-233 0397

December 1993

# Media titles available from John Libbey

*Acamedia Research Monographs*

**Satellite Television in Western Europe** (revised edition 1992)
Richard Collins
Hardback ISBN 0 86196 203 6

**Beyond the Berne Convention**
Copyright, Broadcasting and the Single European Market
Vincent Porter
Hardback ISBN 0 86196 267 2

**Nuclear Reactions: A Study in Public Issue Television**
John Corner, Kay Richardson and Natalie Fenton
Hardback ISBN 0 86196 251 6

**Transnationalization of Television in Western Europe**
Preben Sepstrup
Hardback ISBN 0 86196 280 X

**The People's Voice: Local Radio and Television in Europe**
Nick Jankowski, Ole Prehn and James Stappers
Hardback ISBN 0 86196 322 9

**Television and the Gulf War**
David E. Morrison
Hardback ISBN 0 86196 341 5

**Contra-Flow in Global News**
Oliver Boyd Barrett and Daya Kishan Thussu
Hardback ISBN 0 86196 344 X

**CNN World Report: Ted Turner's International News Coup**
Don M. Flournoy
Hardback ISBN 0 86196 359 8

**Small Nations: Big Neighbour**
Roger de la Garde, William Gilsdorf and Ilja Wechselmann
Hardback ISBN 0 86196 343 1

*BBC Annual Research Reviews*

**Annual Review of BBC Broadcasting Research: No XV - 1989**
Paperback ISBN 0 86196 209 5

**Annual Review of BBC Broadcasting Research: No XVI - 1990**
Paperback ISBN 0 86196 265 6

**Annual Review of BBC Broadcasting Research: No XVII - 1991**
Paperback ISBN 0 86196 319 9

**Annual Review of BBC Broadcasting Research: No XVIII - 1992**
Paperback ISBN 0 86196 368 7
Peter Menneer (ed)

*European Media Research Series*

**The New Television in Europe**
Edited by Alessandro Silj
Hardback ISBN 0 86196 361 X

**Media Industry in Europe**
Edited by Antonio Pilati
Paperback ISBN 0 86196 398 9

# Media titles available from John Libbey

**Broadcasting and Audio-visual Policy in the European Single Market**
Richard Collins
Hardback ISBN 0 86196 405 5

**Aid for Cinematographic and Audio-visual Production In Europe**
(published for the Council of Europe)
Jean-Noël Dibie
Hardback ISBN 0 86196 397 0

## BBC World Service

**BBC World Broadcasting Research 1993**
Edited by Graham Mytton
Paperback ISBN 0 86196 400 4

### Broadcasting Standards Council Publications

**A Measure of Uncertainty: The Effects of the Mass Media**
Guy Cumberbatch and Dennis Howitt
Hardback ISBN 0 86196 231 1

**Violence in Television Fiction: Public Opinion and Broadcasting Standards**
David Docherty
Paperback ISBN 0 86196 284 2

**Survivors and the Media**
Ann Shearer
Paperback ISBN 0 86196 332 6

**Taste and Decency in Broadcasting**
Andrea Millwood Hargrave
Paperback ISBN 0 86196 331 8

**A Matter of Manners? – The Limits of Broadcast Language**
Edited by Andrea Millwood Hargrave
Paperback ISBN 0 86196 337 7

**Sex and Sexuality in Broadcasting**
Andrea Millwood Hargrave
Paperback ISBN 0 86196 393 8

### Broadcasting Research Unit Monographs

**Invisible Citizens:**
**British Public Opinion and the Future of Broadcasting**
David E. Morrison
Paperback ISBN 0 86196 111 0

**Keeping Faith? Channel Four and its Audience**
David Docherty, David E. Morrison and Michael Tracey
Paperback ISBN 0 86196 158 7

**Quality in Television –**
**Programmes, Programme-makers, Systems**
Richard Hoggart (ed)
Paperback ISBN 0 86196 237 0

**School Television in Use**
Diana Moses and Paul Croll
Paperback ISBN 0 86196 308 3

# Media titles available from John Libbey

*UNESCO Publications*

**Video World-Wide: An International Study**
Manuel Alvarado (ed)
Paperback ISBN 0 86196 143 9

*University of Manchester Broadcasting Symposium*

**And Now for the BBC ...**
Proceedings of the 22nd Symposium 1991
Nod Miller and Rod Allen (eds)
Paperback ISBN 0 86196 318 0

**It's Live – But Is It Real?**
Proceedings of the 23rd Symposium 1992
Nod Miller and Rod Allen (eds)
Paperback ISBN 0 86196 370 9

*Published in association with*
*The Arts Council*

**Picture This: Media Representations of Visual Art and Artists**
Philip Hayward (ed)
Paperback ISBN 0 86196 126 9

**Culture, Technology and Creativity**
Philip Hayward (ed)
Paperback ISBN 0 86196 266 4

**Parallel Lines: Media Representations of Dance**
Stephanie Jordan & Dave Allen (eds)
Paperback ISBN 0 86196 371 7

**Arts TV: A History of British Arts Television**
John A Walker
Paperback ISBN 0 86196 435 7

*ITC Television Research Monographs*

**Television in Schools**
Robin Moss, Christopher Jones and Barrie Gunter
Hardback ISBN 0 86196 314 8

**Television: The Public's View**
Barrie Gunter and Carmel McLaughlin
Hardback ISBN 0 86196 348 2

**The Reactive Viewer**
Barrie Gunter and Mallory Wober
Hardback ISBN 0 86196 358 X

**Television: The Public's View 1992**
Barrie Gunter and Paul Winstone
Hardback ISBN 0 86196 399 7

# Media titles available from John Libbey

*Reporters Sans Frontières*

**1992 Report**
Freedom of the Press Throughout the World
Paperback ISBN 0 86196 369 5

**1993 Report**
Paperback ISBN 0 86196 403 9


*IBA Television Research Monographs*

**Teachers and Television:**
**A History of the IBA's Educational Fellowship Scheme**
Josephine Langham
Hardback ISBN 0 86196 264 8

**Godwatching: Viewers, Religion and Television**
Michael Svennevig, Ian Haldane, Sharon Spiers and Barrie Gunter
Hardback ISBN 0 86196 198 6
Paperback ISBN 0 86196 199 4

**Violence on Television: What the Viewers Think**
Barrie Gunter and Mallory Wober
Hardback ISBN 0 86196 171 4
Paperback ISBN 0 86196 172 2

**Home Video and the Changing Nature of Television Audience**
Mark Levy and Barrie Gunter
Hardback ISBN 0 86196 175 7
Paperback ISBN 0 86196 188 9

**Patterns of Teletext Use in the UK**
Bradley S. Greenberg and Carolyn A. Lin
Hardback ISBN 0 86196 174 9
Paperback ISBN 0 86196 187 0

**Attitudes to Broadcasting Over the Years**
Barrie Gunter and Michael Svennevig
Hardback ISBN 0 86196 173 0
Paperback ISBN 0 86196 184 6

**Television and Sex Role Stereotyping**
Barrie Gunter
Hardback ISBN 0 86196 095 5
Paperback ISBN 0 86196 098 X

**Television and the Fear of Crime**
Barrie Gunter
Hardback ISBN 0 86196 118 8
Paperback ISBN 0 86196 119 6

**Behind and in Front of the Screen – Television's Involvement with Family Life**
Barrie Gunter and Michael Svennevig
Hardback ISBN 0 86196 123 4
Paperback ISBN 0 86196 124 2